CLAP YOUR HANDS!

CLAP YOUR HANDS!

by Larry Tomczak

LOGOS INTERNATIONAL
Plainfield, New Jersey 07060

Library of Congress Catalog Card Number: 73–88241
International Standard Book Number: 0–88270–072–3 (Cloth);
0–88270–073–1 (Paper)
Copyright © 1973 by Logos International
All Rights Reserved
Printed in the United States of America

Nihil Obstat:
Reverend Michael J. Arrowsmith, S.T.L.
Censor Deputatus

Imprimatur:
The Most Reverend William W. Baum, S. T. D.
Archbishop of Washington

October 6, 1973

The Nihil Obstat and Imprimatur are official declarations that a book or pamphlet is free of doctrinal or moral error. No implication is contained therein that those who have granted the Nihil Obstat and Imprimatur agree with the content, opinions or statements expressed.

To all who prayed, "Lord, bless Larry and the book."

CLAP YOUR HANDS!

CHAPTER

1

SQUIRMING through the crowd of spectators, I lowered my head, lunged forward, and grabbed the President by the wrist.

"Mr. President, do you read this book?"

His eyes followed my finger as I pointed to the large black Bible in my left hand.

Somewhat taken aback, President Nixon asked me to repeat the question.

"Mr. President, do you read the Bible?"

The smile he tried to swallow got away and slid across his face.

"Young man, I not only read it, but I sometimes even quote from it!"

"Thank you, sir."

The Chief Executive and his entourage resumed their movement toward the White House, and the swelling lunch-hour crowd brushed by me in eager pursuit of a glimpse, a handclasp, maybe even an autograph.

Spring of '72—the country still vibrating from the attempted assassination of Governor Wallace, and there, on the other side of the wrought-iron gate, the Executive Mansion stood powerful and serene, looking exactly as it did on all the postcards. I could scarcely believe I was standing there and could not believe what had just taken place.

I ran my finger along a bar of the fence and smiled. Tonight

I would call Mom back home, and she would say, "What did you do today?"

"Oh, I talked with the President for a while . . ."

Ha! Me, a twenty-three-year-old Polish kid from Euclid, Ohio!

Yet, the hardest thing of all to believe was *what* I had talked to him about . . . and what had happened to my life in so short a time.

Very much alone, I stood there, vaguely aware of the first blaring notes of the afternoon traffic jam. I could not believe the whole thing . . . my life before, and my life after.

I was born in Cleveland, Ohio, in 1949. My mother, Sophie, had not been blessed with the beauty of her two younger sisters, and by her mid-thirties had reconciled herself to single life as a cashier in a downtown department store. But suddenly World War II was over, and many servicemen came home with uncashed warbonds and a hunger to get married and settle down. Stanley Tomczak was one of them—5'10", 200 pounds, proud and Polish, and looking for a nice Catholic Polish girl. On July 4, 1946, Stanley and Sophie became man and wife.

The first really big thing that I remember happened in 1954. That was the year that rock'n'roll was born, as Bill Haley and the Comets tore through "Shake, Rattle and Roll" in black and white saddle shoes. It was also the year that Mom and Dad decided the time had come to find a "decent" home and neighborhood in which to raise six-year-old Margaret and me.

On the fourth of July, our family moved from our timeworn rented home on 96th Street in Cleveland to the comparative suburb of Euclid, where our little white house with the little white fence in front on 200th Street was a dream come true for Mom and Dad. Even the two beer parlors directly across the street couldn't mar the picture—for the time being, at least.

The first day that I walked down our broad tree-lined street, with its neatly manicured lawns and snug, closely-knit suburban homes, I felt I was in a different world. The corner drugstore, the neighborhood delicatessens, and even the many service stations were all kept spic-and-span. Euclid was hardly a posh community, but everyone was obviously expected to "keep up their home" within the standards of suburban respectability.

With a potpourri of ethnic backgrounds, Euclid was a community that was stable, loyal, and closed. The residents were a warm, industrious people who shared common aspirations and basically the same fundamental values about their lives. Most of the families were religious, and a great many expressed their faith in the local Roman Catholic church.

Holy Cross Church was easily seen from the sidewalk in front of our house. Situated two long blocks away, it sat on the corner like an aging mother hen on a barnyard fence, her watchful eye constantly surveying her brood. The large brown brick church was backed up by the large red brick school, while across the street was the convent which housed the Ursuline nuns.

Ours was a good, Polish Catholic family. Dad, who came to America at an early age, disliked it when someone called him an immigrant; anything less than "Polish American" was offensive to him. A religious man, Dad had deep pride in his Catholicism and always insisted on our worshiping together as a family. If there was ever any objection to this or any other of Dad's rules, out came the razor strop. Pop felt that the best way to straighten kids out was to bend them over, and when he got all his weight behind it, he could pack an awful wallop.

Discipline under our roof was a responsibility Mom shared with Dad. She never hesitated to administer a spanking but differed from Dad in that she always delivered a few stern warnings first. A very devout Catholic with strong convictions,

Mom wanted us kids to respect her as a firm but fair parent. "You may not appreciate me now," she would say, "but one day you'll thank me for the way I raised you."

Dad and Mom were strict, but that didn't in any way diminish our deep love for them. Many times I remember crawling up on their bed on Sunday morning and saying, "I love you," while tickling Dad's oversized tummy. Or awakening around midnight during a fearful thunderstorm and hugging Mom during her words of reassurance—"It's just the angels in heaven moving furniture."

Margaret and I fought quite a bit, but we, too, had a strong love for each other. Because she was overweight, I called her "Blimpo," but the only time I used the nickname was when she did something atrocious, like knocking over my carefully arranged plastic soldiers or hiding my favorite baseball card.

Margaret was one person whom I could trust, and only once did she ever betray my confidence. That was when I went to her and asked her about the origin of babies. On the way to kindergarten one day my five-year-old friend, Chucky, had told me that mommies and daddies rub their bellybuttons together to make a baby. Intrigued by such a revelation, I sought my big sister's counsel. She didn't tell *me* anything, but she did tell Mom. What followed was a ten-minute discussion with Dad and a picture-book story about the development of a baby chicken in an egg. That was to be the only formal sex education I would ever receive.

As for church, Dad was active at Holy Cross as an usher and a member of the men's parish organization, the Holy Name Society. During the annual Thanksgiving Festival, Stanley Tomczak, a bright orange apron wrapped around his waist, could be heard well above the crowd. "Lay your money down on a lucky number and win a turkey!"

Mom was an officer in the Court of Mary, the women's counterpart of the Holy Name Society, as well as a faithful volunteer for selling raffle tickets, contributing to bake sales, or pitching in at any of the numerous parish activities. A special affinity for nuns left Mom unable to refuse whenever one of the Sisters called for volunteers.

As for Margaret and me, it was all very grown-up and remote for us, though from the earliest age, we were taught to pray for our vocations in life. Mother would often say how blessed and happy she would be if either of us made a decision to enter the religious life. Margaret a nun? Me a priest? The idea seemed exciting to both of us.

Kneeling down beside our beds each night, Margaret and I would make our petitions known to God and conclude by saying along with Mom and Dad,

> Now I lay me down to sleep
> I pray the Lord my soul to keep;
> If I should die before I wake,
> I pray the Lord my soul to take.

In 1955, at the age of six, I was enrolled at Holy Cross Parochial School. Since Margaret was a year ahead of me, she was able to brief me on what to expect my first day.

"Don't be scared when you see the troops of nuns coming out into the school yard to get you," Margaret instructed. "They'll look like a flock of penguins, but don't let them hear you call them that!"

The adjustment to school was certainly easier with such sage advice, and grades one to four were fun and even exciting to me. But by the time I entered the fifth grade at age ten, I had begun to ask questions that disclosed some pretty deep feelings of inferiority.

Why did I have to have parents who were so old? Dad and Mom were almost fifty. They looked so much older than the parents of my friends that I was extremely self-conscious about them. While my friends' dads often took them to the park for a game of baseball or touch football, my dad always excused himself: "Well, you know, I'm not a young man anymore."

More and more, I began to harbor resentment against my parents; our family, I was convinced, was not as good as anybody else's.

For instance, all my buddies' parents had a car, and most of them had two. Tearfully I'd ask my parents, "Why can't we buy a car? Why do we always have to take those stupid buses?"

On early Sunday morning television, I would watch the ninety-nine-dollar used car specials, and I'd imagine our family inside. Dashing for the kitchen where Mom and Dad would be finishing up breakfast (usually Grandpa's homemade Kielbasa), I'd rattle off the make, year, and "once-in-a-lifetime" price.

"We can't afford it, Larry."

"Why?"

"We can't afford it, Larry!"

I'd pull my Davey Crockett cap over my eyes and leave the kitchen mumbling, "Why do we have to be the only family in Euclid without a car?"

Deep down inside, I knew why we couldn't afford a car: Dad was out of work too often. His age and lack of education were working against him, and when layoffs came, he was always first to go. One month, he'd be doing piecework in a factory, the next, cooking food in a restaurant. Between jobs, to my acute embarrassment, he'd often do yard work for our relatives.

One morning Dad walked eight miles to his niece Estelle's to get her home ready for the winter season and then made the return trip that evening with a ten-dollar bill carefully tucked in his pocket. He never got intoxicated, used foul language, or caused trouble on a job; he was just a little older and a little less skilled and less educated than most employers desired.

When I was eleven, my father got a job on the assembly line at the Ford Motor Company on Cleveland's West Side. One Saturday, he had to make a special trip to the plant, and he asked me if I wanted to go with him. It took a total of three buses and over a mile of walking before we arrived at the massive plant—door to door, about an hour and a half. I recall asking Dad about every fifteen minutes along the way, "How much further is it?" Dad would just smile and chide me for "pooping out."

Although it made no impression on me then, years later I would vividly retrace our steps in my mind as I began to realize just how much my father was doing for our family to survive. Yet at the time, all I could think was that Paul's father was an attorney, Eddie's was vice-president of an engineering firm, my own Uncle Bob was vice-president of a construction company, Uncle Ben was president and founder of a bank, but to me my dad was a "failure," about to be laid off work for the seventh time. Even though my buddies would say, "You manage to make it—you're living as good as us," deep down inside I knew it wasn't true.

They had a car. Their dads had good jobs. Their families went on vacations. Their parents were young. They'd get a steak once a week—for us, it was four times a year on our birthdays.

Preferring not to be seen in the presence of my parents, I avoided them as much as possible. But Holy Cross parish invariably seemed to bring the four of us together as a family. Initially, it was only for Sunday and holy day Masses, but something else was about to happen.

One Friday, as our family sat down for the usual fish dinner, Mom refrained from putting the food on the table right away. I was just about to complain about the delay, when Mom bowed her head and began to say grace—"Bless us, oh Lord, in these Thy gifts which we are about to receive, from Thy bounty through Christ our Lord. Amen.

"Before I bring the food out," Mom continued, "I'd like to say something."

"Can't you dish the food out and *then* talk?" I whined. "Mom, I'm starving."

"This won't take long. You kids know that your father has been out of work for three months during the strike, and it hasn't been easy to make ends meet. So we've decided something that seems to be our only answer for keeping food on this table."

"We're not going to move?" Margaret interjected.

"No, Margaret. But I'm going to take a job while Dad is looking for work."

"What?" we chorused. "Where?"

"The Sisters at Holy Cross have offered me a job cleaning in their convent on Fridays and washing and waxing the classroom floors in the school on Saturdays. It'll bring in twenty dollars a week."

Margaret and I nodded reluctant approval and then reached for the fish. The news surprised us both because Mom, who had been born without a right hip socket and could never walk without pain, now had acute arthritis in her right hip as well. Lately her limp was becoming more pronounced, and she had been promising to see a doctor.

But for me, the real letdown was not so much the job itself but the location. That was all I needed! Now all the kids at school would see my mother—with a scrub-bucket!

As if that wasn't bad enough, a few months later, Mom got still another cleaning job—this one in the 200th Street Medical Building, directly across the street from school! Anyone who'd look in from the street could easily see Mrs. Tomczak, "Larry's mother," down on all fours, making everything spotless.

The time I hated most was after school when Mom would wait for me on the corner. No sixth grade guy liked having to hang around his mother when he was almost a teenager, especially when she was a "scrubwoman." Often I'd ask Sister if I could empty the wastebaskets after school, just to avoid the ten-minute promenade down East 200th Street with Mom. More than half the students at Holy Cross filed down this street on their way home, and helping to carry Mom's cleaning supplies while she limped alongside me was more than I could bear.

"Larry, your *Mommy* is waiting for you on the corner!" some of the guys would jeer as our class filed neatly out of school with Sister leading the troop.

"Aw, shut up!" was about all I could muster.

All during my sixth and seventh grades at Holy Cross, Mom continued her three jobs. Dad found sporadic employment, but nothing permanent. He kept looking.

Near the end of my seventh year at Holy Cross, I began to notice how Mom seemed to be struggling more each day, how difficult it was for her just to walk. Kneeling on cold concrete floors for more than twenty hours a week was taking its toll. Mom refused to use a mop, saying she just couldn't do as good a job standing up. She borrowed a whirlpool machine for the bathtub and applied liniment morning and night, but neither treatment alleviated the pain. A support-cane brought little relief, and finally she was forced to take pain-killers twice a day to help her endure the throbbing.

"Mother?" I'd whisper, as I gently pushed open her bedroom door. Lying on her stomach with a heating pad on her hip and the covers pulled almost over her head, Mom would be crying.

"Mom, can I get you anything?"

Sniffling under the covers, she gave her usual answer—"Larry, would you say a prayer for me, please?"

"Okay, Mom."

Closing the door, I'd go back into my room saying, "Jesus, Mary, and Joseph, help Mom. Jesus, Mary, and Joseph, help Mom . . ."

An operation was the only recourse. The doctors told her they would have to insert a synthetic ball joint into her deteriorated hip to try to relieve some of the pain. The surgery would take over nine hours.

Finally a date was set for the operation, and Mom was

forced to give up her jobs. At least she wouldn't be near school anymore. But what happened? Dad took over both positions. By the time Dad finally got a steady job as a custodian at a nearby bank, where he still works today, I had mentally disowned both my parents.

In the eighth grade, desperate for something to compensate for the obvious injustice in my life, I ran for class president—and was elected. The position provided me with the sense of importance that I craved; the void in my life had been filled. But it wasn't to last very long.

CHAPTER

2

TAPPING the long, wooden pointer on her desktop, Sister Eileen gently prodded our first grade class.

"Why did God make us?"

In ragged unison, our entire class would recite in angelic simplicity, "God made us to know, love, and serve Him in this world."

Parochial school . . . collecting the milk money and clapping out the erasers . . . slipping out my Pez candy dispenser while Sister's back was turned . . . writing "J.M.J." (Jesus, Mary, and Joseph) on top of the paper . . . singing for the May crownings . . . reading book after book on the lives of the saints . . . collecting the canned goods for the Thanksgiving baskets . . . counting the days till CYO (Catholic Youth Organization) camp opened . . .

Holy Cross was a stable parish community of about two thousand. Here was where we came for Mass, baptism, confirmation, weddings, funerals, raffles, bake sales, and clothing drives. Here we scurried to the confession box with our sins and then later approached the altar rail for Communion. Here we came for the novenas and forty-hours' devotion. And here we deposited our collection envelopes for the support of our Holy Mother, the Church.

For a first and second grader, "Holy Mother" was indeed

11

appropriate. A catechism answer correctly stated from memory assured me of "Mother's" stamp of approval—a red, blue, or gold star affixed to my forehead. Answering all five questions correctly meant the acquisition of a "specially" blessed medal of the Blessed Virgin Mary or maybe a "holy card" portraying Saint Francis of Assisi and all his little animal friends. Everything was so simple then. Holy Mother, the Church, knew what was best for me, and all I had to do was be obedient.

But in the third grade, things started to change. I began asking questions. I had to; there was too much I didn't understand.

Standing mid-center in our darkened church, I reverently genuflected, slipped into pew number twenty-one, and let down the kneeler—carefully, to avoid that terrible thump. The sun's rays seeped soft, warm through the numerous stained-glass windows. Lifting my eyes, I noticed the corpus on the crucifix was hidden under a mysterious purple cloak. No need for alarm; Jesus had not been stolen, only concealed, for it was the season of Lent.

Although the Lenten period lasted only forty days and then the cloak was lifted, Jesus Christ would still remain hidden to me. A patterned response in our catechism labeled Him as "the only begotten Son of God," but just what did that mean?

God seemed so rigid. How many times I remember walking solemnly down the center aisle in church to the communion rail. Filing upward in orderly lines, we were always tense, for the eyes of Sister might be on us. Eyes were downcast, following the shuffling little feet before us. Hands were folded, pointing upward to heaven.

Kneeling at the communion rail, my mouth dry from fasting, I'd be given a taste of God on my tongue. "Don't chew the host, or you'll chew the baby Jesus!" Sister had sternly warned. I would bow my head and begin the countdown: "One thousand one, one thousand two, one thousand three." Then I would stand to file back to the pew. Always on the way back I would peek up at the kids who had not gone forward for Communion and conjecture what mortal sin they must have committed.

Entering the pew, I would realize that I had forgotten to genuflect. Quickly, before Sister saw, I'd backtrack a step into the aisle, turn to the altar, bend my right knee to the floor alongside the ankle of the left foot, hold my head and the upper part of my body erect, rise again without delay, and hurriedly slip back into place.

As a nine-year-old fourth grader, I felt God becoming more mysterious. During forty-hours' devotion, a period of time set aside yearly by each parish for special prayer and various acts of worship, I would file neatly down the center aisle with the five hundred other students. Our eyes were glued to the elderly nun who stood directly before us. Hundreds of adults, already seated, turned their heads to survey our orderly procession. Looks of disapproval came from some of the older women as they noted the "disrespectful" girls who had forgotten a covering for their heads. At just the precise moment, as Sister lowered her head, the girls separated from their boy partners and filed into the pews—girls on the left and boys on the right. Latecomers would have to stand in the side aisles; Holy Cross Church was filled to capacity.

The altar, covered in gleaming linen in the middle of the sanctuary, was surrounded by acolytes kneeling around our four parish priests, robed in black vestments. After ten minutes of liturgical chants and fifteen minutes of prayer responses, the organ music stopped abruptly and a deep hush came over the congregation. No one in church dared to cough. Incense permeated the air. The only movement inside Holy Cross Church seemed to be the blood-red vigil candles fluttering under the statues.

Father McMonagle, our elderly gray-haired pastor, solemnly ascended the carpeted steps to the marble altar. His back to the congregation, he genuflected three times, and proceeded to unlock the little doors of the golden tabernacle on the altar. Pulling his silken vestment over his hands so as not to touch anything directly, Father McMonagle slowly turned around holding the sacred gold object called the Monstrance. As smoke from the incense holders floated around him, Father held the object out at arms' length directly in front of him. He turned once to the right, once to the left, and then back to mid-center. The gold Monstrance was clearly in view for everyone. In a trembling voice, the boy next to me leaned his body against mine and whispered, "That's Jesus!"

The Monstrance was then placed on the altar to stay throughout the forty-hours' devotion. I asked one of the Sisters, "Why is it so holy? What's so special about it?" The reply came quickly, "Jesus is inside there."

I asked Mom over and over, "How can He be in there?" Mom's reply was always the same: "It's a mystery. Don't ask silly questions. You just go and pay a visit to Jesus while He's 'exposed' on the altar."

So I'd wander into church in the middle of the afternoon, remove my baseball cap, carefully make the sign of the cross with holy water, genuflect (always on *two* knees when Jesus was exposed) and then kneel down in the last pew, staring intently at that object on the altar. Finally, when everybody had left the church but me, I would walk apprehensively down the long, freshly waxed center aisle to get a closer look. I knelt down at the communion rail with my head bowed. Slowly I lifted my head, opened my eyes, and squinted at the small window in the center of the object. Straining my eyes, I tried to see inside. It was no use—the glass was tinted brown, and the window was too small. Saying an "Our Father, Hail Mary, and Glory be," I'd stand, genuflect, and exit from the church, still disappointed.

God seemed so elusive— Was Jesus in the communion host? Was He in that gold object? Was He only in church?

Why did God have to be so hard to contact? As a Catholic, I had my miniature plastic statues, rosary, and Saint Joseph missal. I had always been taught to pray *to* something, *with* something, or *from* something. Could God be approached directly? Did He really prefer that we address Him in Latin? Was my pig latin just as good?

At times it seemed that God preferred to stay out of the picture, and I had a hard time keeping track of everyone to whom I was to go when in need. My personal needs could be handled easily by my guardian angel. Saint Lawrence was my patron saint, and he knew all my "special" needs. Saint Christopher handled travel—even my bike had the blessed medal on the handlebars; Saint Jude Thaddeus took my "impossible cases"; Saint Joseph of Cupertino minded my scholastic activities; Saint Theresa, the Little Flower, took care of all those impure thoughts, words, and desires; the saint whose feast was listed on our calendar for the day always had "extra" graces to bestow; and so it went.

Of course I could never fail to mention my Heavenly Mother, Mary. The universal exhortation could not be forgotten: "You ask Mary because you know that when you want something from your earthly father you always go to your mother first and she takes care of it for you."

And when I sinned, I always had a priest to whom I could go. Many times I waited in the extra-long confessional lines, because word had gotten around that "Father so-and-so asks fewer questions than the other priests."

Thursday mornings meant confession when I was in the seventh grade, a chance to meet Christ in His sacrament of love and forgiveness—a fact, not yet readily perceived at this early age.

Neatly regimented into the pews in the side chapels of the church, our class of thirty knelt down, examined our consciences, and when ready, filed into a line to await a turn in the confession box. Silence prevailed, with the only sounds coming from the rear of the church where some grandmothers were individually praying their rosaries in audible whispers.

All of a sudden, the tranquillity of the church was shattered. "You *what?*" bellowed a priestly voice from the confession box that I had avoided.

Oh, no, I thought, Denny's really going to get it—I told him not to go in that line.

Within ten seconds, five of my classmates had slipped out of that line and moved over into my line.

A chorus of disjointed coughing immediately arose from the chapel. "Whenever someone's voice can be overheard from the confessional," Sister had admonished us, "cough or make some other distracting noise so no one can hear what is said. If you don't, you will have to confess to the priest that you were *eavesdropping* on someone's confession. Is that clear?"

Above the confessional door were two lights—when the top bulb was lit, a priest was in the confessional; when the lower bulb was lit, a person had depressed the kneeler inside the box and was making his confession.

As the spasmodic coughing and page-turning continued, I noticed that the lower light was periodically blinking off and on, yet the door was staying closed. Peering through the frosted glass on the confessional door, I could see only the faint outline of Denny's head.

Boy, Denny sure has been in there a long time, I thought, as I glanced at my watch.

Finally, about fifteen minutes after he went in, my small friend slowly pushed open the huge confessional door and emerged, eyes downcast and face pale. His glasses even appeared to be steamed.

Must have committed a mortal sin, I decided.

When my turn for confession came, I walked into the box, knelt down, made the sign of the cross, said, "Bless me, Father, for I have sinned," enumerated my sins, asked forgiveness, accepted my penance (recitation of three "Our Fathers" and three "Hail Marys") and exited. I always tried to keep my time in the confessional under three minutes. That way, no one got suspicious.

Emerging from the confessional, I noticed a space in the pew next to Denny. Kneeling down next to him, I cupped my hands in a repentant manner over my face and began my penance: "Hail Mary, full of grace . . ." When I had finished, I kept my hands over my face and leaned close to Denny.

"Psst!"

"Huh?" Denny responded, as he casually turned to check the clock in the back of the church and see if Sister was watching.

Lowering my voice to a barely audible whisper, I said, "The priest really worked you over, huh?"

"Nah," Denny retorted, with a sureness I couldn't help admiring.

"You're not in any trouble, are you?"

"Nah."

"Well, what the heck happened in there? Man, you were in there forever. Even Sister was wondering, especially when the confessional light started shorting out."

Denny jerked his head. "Oh, no!" He almost shouted. "Was that stupid confessional light blinking on and off?"

"Yeah," I said. "What was going on? What were you—"

"Ah-hem!" came from Sister Angela a few rows behind us, giving us her usual throat-clearing warning.

Resuming an erect position, we moved apart and feigned prayer.

A few minutes later, Sister Angela swept by us (the wind created by her starched habit was always refreshing on hot days) and went up front to talk to another nun.

"Hurry up," I said, tugging Denny's sleeve. "What happened?"

He leaned close to me. "All week long I've been dreading going to confession because of an impure sin I committed.

When I finally managed enough courage to confess it, Father said, 'You what?' so loud that—"

"Yeah, everyone heard him!" I interrupted.

"That's what I was afraid of! I panicked, and when he dismissed me, I was scared to come out! I didn't know what to do. I was stuck. So I squatted back off the kneeler onto my heels for a few seconds and then knelt again. I disguised my voice and said, 'Bless me, Father, for I have sinned,' and then made up a whole new batch of sins. He didn't even know the difference. Only thing I goofed was forgetting about that dumb light."

"Are you serious?" I said, dumbfounded. "How many times did you do that?"

"Five," Denny said.

"What made you finally stop? Did you settle down enough to come out?"

"Nah, not really; I just ran out of sins."

As a thirteen-year-old eighth grader about to proceed on to high school, I had a mountain of questions stored up in my mind. Increasingly, God was ceasing to exist as any kind of reality for me. In newspaper articles and on bumper stickers, I kept seeing the words, "God is dead." Every time I saw them, I'd tell myself, "But there's got to be a God. How can there be a creation without a Creator?"

I tried hard to picture God as alive, vibrant, and above all, responsive. His rigidity and mystery could be tolerated; being elusive, hard to contact, and remote were understandable, considering the millions under His care; but why didn't He want me to feel He was living and existing for right now? Why the constant emphasis on the lifeless and moribund? Christmas and Easter meant a lot to me—they brought God back to life, and provided hope and expectation—but why couldn't we sense it the rest of the year?

The harder I tried to visualize God as alive and real, the

more evidence I seemed to be getting to the contrary. Whether I was in church for Mass or confession or choir practice or just a visit, one thing always dominated my perspective. Directly above the altar was a larger-than-life Jesus Christ on a massive cross. Arms outstretched and body languid, *Jesus Christ was dead.*

Frozen in my position as an altar boy in the sanctuary, I would often find myself mesmerized by the crucifix as I knelt, scarce inches below Christ's feet. The blood from the wounds in His hands and feet and side appeared to be almost warm.

In every classroom in Holy Cross School, a large crucifix hung just above the front blackboard. Each one of the Ursuline nuns who taught us wore a large black crucifix around her neck. And in every corridor of the school were hung pictures of the crucifixion.

"Now you kneel there before that crucifix for one hour, young man, and you just think about the sufferings that Jesus endured on that cross!"

How often I remember those words, as Sister meted out punishment for misbehavior. I'd kneel, fidgeting from left knee to right, staring at the crucified body of Jesus.

And then there were the Stations of the Cross—retracing Christ's steps from Pilate's condemnation to His death on Calvary. Why did we have to finish with Jesus still dead?

Every time I attended Mass, I joined the congregation in reciting the Apostles' Creed from a printed Mass card. But I didn't understand it.

What does it mean, "descended into hell," I would wonder. Or, "from thence He shall come to judge the living and the dead"? And what is this line—"the resurrection of the body"?

I'd look around at the grown-ups at Mass on Sunday and wonder how many of them really knew what they were saying.

"I believe in God, the Father Almighty, Creator of heaven and earth, and in Jesus Christ His only Son, our Lord, who was conceived by the Holy Spirit, born of the Virgin Mary, suffered under Pontius Pilate, was crucified, died and was buried. He descended into hell. The third day . . ."

I would lower my voice to a whisper, close my eyes, and proceed at my own pace, as I tried to concentrate—

"He *arose* from the dead,

He *ascended* into heaven,

He *now* sits at the right hand of God . . . from thence He shall come to judge the living and the dead. I believe in the Holy Spirit, the Holy Catholic Church (what's going to happen to all the Protestants? I'd often wonder), the communion of saints, the forgiveness of sins, the resurrection of the body, and life everlasting. Amen."

As the congregation knelt, I repeated the words again under my breath—

"He *arose* from the dead,

He *ascended* into heaven,

He *now* sits at the right hand of God . . ."

You are there somewhere, aren't You, God?

This was where my thinking was at the end of grade school. But confusion about God was not all that preoccupied my thoughts. I had been taught that I had a soul, and that my soul was going to spend eternity somewhere. That meant, as Sister put it, "forever and *ever*." Although I had not the slightest idea what my soul looked like, I definitely wanted to spend forever and *ever* in the right place.

There were endless rules, rituals, and regulations that I had to adhere to in order to get my soul into what our catechism called, "that place where we see God face to face."

Many of the requirements confused me, but there were two tenets that I knew for certain. No one could graduate from a parochial school without understanding the two basic ground rules listed in our catechism:

(1) Only those with grace on their soul at the moment of death would go to heaven.

(2) The result of sin was punishment. Serious sin (mortal) left on the soul at death sent one to hell, a place of everlasting punishment. Other sins (venial) sent the soul to Purgatory, a place of temporary punishment, where the soul was cleansed of sin and then forwarded to heaven.

In line with the first ground rule, I recall quite explicitly the exhortation of our catechism: "Therefore our time on earth should be spent in gaining as much grace as possible." Having a strong competitive nature, I was determined not merely to earn my way into heaven but to assure myself of that "greater happiness." Grace was needed to get into heaven, but the more grace I had, the more happiness I was assured of, once I was there. The formula was simple: the more grace on a soul, the more clearly one would see God.

Through the sacraments, prayer, the route of First Fridays consecutively attended (miss one and you'd have to start again), and good works, I was able to gain grace. Often after receiving Holy Communion or dropping my loose change in the church poor box, I envisioned God's mighty finger depressing the keys on His heavenly adding machine. A few times in the fifth grade, I lit some vigil candles after depositing slugs in the metal coin box but soon quit after realizing that Mr. Schmidt, the custodian, wasn't the only one who knew what went into the box. What if God started subtracting from my totals!

And so on it went, grace stored upon grace. How much grace it took to merit heaven I did not know. The instructions were to "gain as much grace as possible," and that was exactly what I set out to do.

Yet, always, in the back of my mind there was that one thing that could take away all the grace that I had in storage. It was the same thing that could send me to hell forever and *ever*—that ominous, sinister bogeyman of every young Catholic, spiritual enemy number one, the epitome of evil—*Mortal Sin*.

That phrase—*Mortal Sin*—sounded so wicked and diabolic, so dirty and wretched and frightening. It looked even worse in our catechism.

Question 4: What is mortal sin?

Response: Mortal sin is a *big* sin; a serious violation of God's law.

Examples: murder, adultery, willfully failing to assist at Mass on all Sundays and holy days of obligation.

Question 5: What does mortal sin do to the soul?

Response: It kills the grace in your soul.

Question 6: Where will you go if you die with a mortal sin on your soul?

Response: You will go to hell *forever*.

With a sword like that hanging over my head, I strove to do all I could to avoid sin and the possibility of going to hell.

Never, not even once, did I question the existence of hell. How could I? From the time I entered first grade all the way through the eighth, hell and the possibility of ending up in that "fiery pit of torment" were vital parts of my spiritual education. Whenever someone said, "Go to hell," during one of the touch football games that we played on the asphalt alongside the school, I would recall what one of the nuns had said as she pointed her finger at our class: "You'd better not say that, or God might punish you by saying it to *you* one day!"

Mortal sin was like a burglar in that it robbed one's spiritual treasury of all its stored grace. Imagine years and years of accumulated grace going down the drain because of one slip-up! Many times I shuddered at the possibility of being mowed down by a passing bus or incurring a premature heart attack before I could up-date my confession.

One precautionary measure against spending eternity in hell was to resist temptation, especially those dreadful "occasions of sin" (persons, places, or things that could lead me to fall). It certainly wasn't easy, because one could never really be sure how far one could go before temptation ceased and sin began.

"Kissing a girl is almost always an occasion of sin," said Father, as his index finger tapped the desk in front of the class. Because of a series of "scandalous" holiday parties, Sister Mary had called in one of our middle-aged priests to talk to our eighth grade class. It was late Friday afternoon, and the dismissal bell was about to ring. All thirty of us sat in a respectful manner with hands folded atop the books that were piled on our desks. After every other sentence of Father's, I shifted my eyes to the second hand on the wall clock. Pacing back and forth in front of the classroom, Father—in his ankle-length black cassock—was the symbol of religious authority at Holy Cross.

"It has been brought to my attention," Father said, "that some—and I'm not saying all—but *some* of you students have been getting involved in some questionable activities. You know perfectly well what I'm talking about.

"Now let's be honest with ourselves: young boys and girls have something in their natures which attracts them to one another." Heads out of his line of vision nodded in agreement. "God gave you that attraction for a good purpose. But that attraction becomes dangerous when it is used for selfish pleasure. That's why petting, embracing, and kissing must be avoided. They are clear-cut occasions of sin. They tend to arouse feelings of passion which lead from one liberty to another and frequently into mortal sin."

Mortal sin. There was that word again. I winced. Maybe it wasn't so bad that Mom didn't allow me to go to those parties.

Father was still talking. "I know what you're saying to yourselves now: Oh, I know when to stop. That's what *you* say! Our Holy Father has been warning the nations against just such lustful attitudes.

"Catholic boys and girls must *never* allow themselves to become playthings for others' pleasure.

"Now I'm going to recommend that you do four things from now on to strengthen yourselves against indecent temptations:

"First, avoid all those persons, places, actions, and things that might lead you into sin.

"Second, pray to God and His Blessed Mother for protection. Three Hail Marys daily in honor of Our Lady of Purity would be best.

"Thirdly, practice mortification of your senses. Do something hard every day for love of God.

"Finally—this one is primarily for the boys—don't do *anything* with a girl that you would be ashamed to do in the presence of your mother."

Ring!

Three-thirty, time to go home. Everyone started to get up and talk, when Father interrupted. "Hold it, right there! Before you stand for dismissal prayer, I want to mention one final thing that you can reflect on tonight."

Waiting for the murmuring to stop, Father continued: "A few years ago, a young couple that I knew were parked down at Neff Road Park, and the young man got a little too intimate with his girl friend. Later that night, around midnight, he was struck by lightning—and *its fire burned the sign of the cross into his chest.*"

While our mouths hung open, Father gave us a quick blessing and left us to examine our consciences before going home for the weekend.

Another precautionary measure against going to hell was to avoid the venial sins which "so easily could lead a boy or girl to bigger and bigger sins." What made it more difficult was the fact that if one didn't know whether something was a mortal or venial sin, the instruction came loud and clear—"*Do not do it!* Otherwise you will commit a mortal sin because you show yourself willing to offend God seriously."

Still another precautionary measure I applied in trying to avoid hell, was to remove, while still here on earth, as much as possible of the punishment due to my sins. Even though I confessed my sins to a priest, and the sins were forgiven, God, I was instructed, still demanded that I be punished for my sins. This punishment was called "temporal (temporary) punishment," and it was inflicted on my soul in that place where the soul was cleansed for heaven—Purgatory. Besides not being able to see God face to face, the souls in Purgatory suffered a great deal as the sins were "burned out." In my mind I would imagine an almost endless assembly line of angels holding long forceps from which dangled souls in transit to heaven. One angel would dip a soul into an open furnace of fire for a designated time and then pass it along to the next angel in line, who repeated the process. With each immersion, more sins in the soul would be dislodged, until what began as a charcoal soul had finally become lily white. When the mission was completed, Archangel Gabriel would personally carry the purified soul to that place where it could "see God face to face."

Besides the obvious desire for a shorter stay in Purgatory, I wanted to remove as much as possible of the temporal punishment in order to maintain a better standing in the sight of God. I figured that the less punishment I had coming, the more God would love me and help me to avoid sin and hell. The two best ways to remove the punishment were doing penance and gaining indulgences.

Works of penance are acts of atonement that one can perform on his own to make satisfaction to God for sin, e.g., fasting and prayer. An indulgence took away all or part of the temporal punishment still due to sin through the intervention of the Church, e.g., using holy water or making the Stations of the Cross both afforded an indulgence.

Works of penance were always slightly easier after Sister
had us read a portion from the writings of Saint Theresa, the
gentle "Little Flower."

"It has been brought to my attention," said the nun who was
my sixth-grade instructor, "that many of you students are
coming to Saturday confessions and leaving the church *before*
you kneel down and say your penance. That is a disgrace!
What kind of example are you setting for the little first and
second graders?"

Sister folded her arms on her freshly starched white habit
and shook her head in disapproval.

"What am I going to do with you? You're eleven and twelve
years old, and some of you haven't grown up a bit since the
day you came to Holy Cross!"

Sister then picked up a book containing biographies of some
of the saints. "On page eighty-eight is a short paragraph
relating the terrifying vision that God granted to Saint Theresa
of the multitudes of souls falling into hell like leaves in
autumn. I want each one of you to read the section and pass it
to the person behind you. Maybe *this* will impress upon your
minds how serious it is when we disobey the laws of God."

Invariably after such a reading, I would find myself first in
line to sign up as a server for the 6:00 A.M. Mass the coming
week. After all, I thought, it will all be worth it when I'm in
heaven sooner than the rest of the guys.

Lent was always the best time to do penance. Sister would
ask our class to be silent for five minutes and decide what
penance we would offer up for the forty-day period of Lent. It
was always quite a competitive event, and usually the last
person's announcement was the highlight of the afternoon.

"Barbara," Sister said, "you go first."

"I'll limit myself to one candy bar a day for Lent."

"Francis?"

"I'll not eat any candy at all."

"Ann?"

"I will not eat any desserts during Lent."

"Mary?"

"I will skip all desserts, too."

"Thomas?"

"I will not eat any dessert *or* watch 'Zorro' for all of Lent."

"Dennis?"

"I will give up *all* desserts, *all* television, *plus* go to Mass and Communion every day."

"Larry?"

It was my turn. Saint Theresa and those autumnal leaves were vivid in my mind. My palms began to perspire as I nervously tapped my pencil box on my desktop.

"Well?" Sister prompted.

Sitting up at my desk, I asserted, "I will spend one hour *each* day saying the rosary and praying before the Blessed Sacrament!"

The fellow behind me groaned under his breath, as Sister continued to call the roll.

I felt I had outsmarted my seventh grade class. While the other students would only be doing penance, I would be gaining indulgences in addition to my penance. It had taken me years to figure out the system, but now I knew how to get the most out of my time and sacrifice. Saying the rosary before the Blessed Sacrament was worth 500 days indulgence. That meant every time I did it, I would have 500 more days removed from my future stay in Purgatory. That would add up to 20,000 days by the end of Lent!

Throughout my grade-school years, I remember trying to determine how many days off my stay in Purgatory I could gain by performing certain acts.

A minimal indulgence (ten days, I think) was given for making the sign of the cross with holy water. Time after time I would stop before leaving church in order to cross myself one hundred times in machine-gun-like fashion. This practice lasted only until about the sixth grade when I realized I could gain just as many indulgences by quickly reciting, "Jesus, Mary, and Joseph—pray for me" one hundred times. I could say it during a television commercial or standing in my left-field position waiting for the next fly ball to come my way.

I used to time myself as I said the rosary in order to see how fast I could rack up a few more years of indulgence. As I finished the last Hail Mary, I would visualize an angel making another deposit in my heavenly bank account for later withdrawal.

Once a year, on November 2, came a feast I anticipated all year long. On All Souls Day, Catholics were able to gain plenary indulgence—one that takes away *all* temporal punishment—for someone in Purgatory. The conditions were relatively easy: Confession, Communion, and a prayer for the Pope.

One afternoon I came home from school, dumped my books on the dining-room table, and sauntered over to the television. It was four o'clock, time for "American Bandstand."

"Larry," Margaret said from the sofa, where she was wrapped in thought, "you know what day it is tomorrow?"

"Wednesday, isn't it?"

Margaret shook her head in disgust. "Not the day of the week, dummy—what's *significant* about tomorrow?"

"I don't know, honest," I said.

Margaret leaned forward and threw up her arms. "Tomorrow is *All Souls Day!*"

"Oh, wow! Man, I'm glad *you* remembered! Have you decided who we are going to take?"

"Well, that's what I was *trying* to do when you so *rudely* turned on the TV. I was trying to think—did we get Grampa Tomczak last year?"

"I don't remember. Check in the back of your missal."

Margaret found her missal and began to flip through the pages until she came to the one where we had recorded the names of certain "select" relatives.

"Here it is." She scanned the page. "We prayed Grampa Tomczak out of Purgatory three years ago. I think you'd better come up with another one this year, and I'll take Mr. Mazee. I doubt if anyone has got him out yet."

"Don't you think we should stick with family?" I asked.

"Look, dummy," Margaret said, heading toward the kitchen, "there's nobody in the family left. We've gotten them all!"

"Yeah," I said, thinking on that. "Just think how many people in heaven will be praying for *us* when *we're* in Purgatory! Man! We'll be set!"

As I looked forward to entering Saint Joseph's High School, I took a summer job as a salesman for the Carmelite Fathers, and for six months went door-to-door selling the Catholic publication, *The Mary*. Along with each new subscription, I would give the person a Brown Scapular as an additional gift. (A scapular consists of two small squares of woolen cloth joined by strings and worn about the neck for devotional purposes.)

In my six months of saleswork, I contacted over a thousand Catholic families, always with a standard, four-minute pitch supplied by my regional sales manager.

"Good morning, ma'am, I'm calling for the Carmelite Fathers. Are you folks Catholic here?"

Our sales manager instructed us to lean forward and smile as we put our opening question. Somewhat caught off balance, the prospect—usually a middle-aged housewife—responded, "Oh, ah, yes, we're Catholics here. Who did you say you're with?"

Broadening my smile, I'd say, "The Carmelite Fathers—the religious order out of Illinois."

"Oh, yes. I think I've heard of them."

That was all I needed. "Well, the Carmelite Fathers are trying to spread devotion to Mary, Our Lady of Mount

Carmel, and they're asking the cooperation of all the Catholic families in the neighborhood."

Unsnapping my official-looking black vinyl satchel, I would pull out an attractive two-fold tract with gold-ruled lines and continue my patter, holding the paper out in front of me.

"The Fathers would like you to fill out this petition, listing on the inside the members of your family, and then on the back, any special intentions that you might be praying for such as world peace or good health in the family. Those are certainly worthwhile intentions, aren't they?"

In asking the question of my prospect, I'd follow another tip given me by the sales manager: "Always nod your head up and down as you ask a question. Apply the 'yes-yes technique' so you'll put your customer in a positive frame of mind. Then it will be much easier to later close your sale."

"Now," I would continue, "the Carmelite Fathers will place this petition on the altar at their seminary and remember all of your prayer intentions every day in their Masses."

Reaching into my satchel again, I'd bring forth the Brown Scapular. It was neatly wound around an accompanying information sheet. As I extended the little packet toward the housewife (Tip number three—How to get your prospect to unlatch the screen), she'd immediately open her door.

"The Fathers would also like someone in your family to have this sacred Brown Scapular; yes, it has *already* been blessed." And I would follow her inside.

"In return, the Fathers are asking for a small enrollment to help spread the devotion." Nodding approvingly once again, I'd smile and say, "Won't you help the boys out?"

The befuddled prospect would then look at me and ask the inevitable question, "Well . . . what am I supposed to do?"

Expanding my smile even further, I'd bring the sale to a close.

"Ma'am, the Fathers want to remember you and your family's intentions in daily Masses for three years; plus, have

...ept, as a *gift*, the Brown Scapular—
...'s promise, 'If anyone dies while
...wearer will never suffer the pains of

...rs want to send along to you a
...n magazine, *The Mary*."

...remove the *Mary Magazine*, which
...*er's Digest*. Then, as quickly as I'd
...f sight. "The enrollment is only five

..., the usual excuses would come
...o at this time." "My husband has
...ady receive a Catholic magazine."

...xcuses, we were well prepared with an arsenal of
"can't miss" sales comebacks that our sales manager himself
had perfected over the years. Sincerity and voice inflection
were the keys to "successfully sealing the sale." My smile now
resembled that of the Cheshire cat.

"Yes . . . but, you know, we can *all* use more prayers, can't
we? God will *surely* bless you and yours for your generosity.
And remember the solemn promise of Mary: 'If anyone dies
while wearing this Scapular, the wearer will *never* . . . *suffer*
. . . *the* . . . *pains* . . . *of* . . . *hell.*"

Unless an irritable husband was at home, the sale would
usually be consummated. With each five-dollar order, I made
two dollars. If I put in a solid eight-hour day, I'd average a
take-home of anywhere between twenty-five to forty dollars.
But since I had a problem with motivation, I usually worked
an hour or two, made ten bucks, then hit a nearby hamburger
stand and goofed off the rest of the day.

Many times I wondered just how much of the five dollars
actually went to "help the boys out," and I had a hard time
visualizing that altar at the seminary and the stacks of petitions
that must have accumulated over the years.

That Brown Scapular was my final precautionary measure

against going to hell. I didn't understand how the Scapular worked, but the Church said that it did, and I believed it.

In leaving Holy Cross Elementary School, I felt that I understood my mission as a Catholic: to gain heaven and avoid hell.

In the end it will all be worth it, I thought. The Catholic Church is a hard one to live in, but a good one to die in.

In June of 1963, five months before the assassination of President Kennedy, I received my diploma from Holy Cross Grade School, my impressions of God and the Roman Catholic Church well established in my mind. I was entering a Catholic high school, but almost seventy percent of my classmates would not continue on to a Catholic secondary school or any further religious instruction. "Where are they now?" is a question I have asked myself a thousand times.

CHAPTER

3

"YOU *are privileged to be a Saint Joseph's 'Viking' and don't you ever forget it!"*

Echoing throughout the huge gymnasium, the authoritative voice of the principal of Saint Joseph's High School evoked immediate silence from our freshman class. Amid the more than five hundred freshmen assembled for the 1963 Orientation Day activities, I sat in the balcony and scanned the auditorium below.

The glow from the giant ceiling lights cast a purple shadow over the crowded tile floor. Now I know why they've nicknamed this place the "Purple Palace," I thought, and boy, talk about enormous! No wonder tuition is two hundred bucks a year.

The basketball court in the center of the gym was covered with row upon row of folding chairs, and the foldaway bleachers along the three side walls had been fully extended to the edge of the court. Only a few vacant seats were visible.

Everyone's attention was directed toward the elevated front stage, above which hung a twenty-foot-long blue banner with red lettering spelling out: "Saint Joseph High School Vikings."

Proud of being a freshman at the largest Catholic boys' high school in Ohio, I felt the strong *esprit de corps* among the student body. But the womb-like security I had experienced among a hundred and twenty classmates at Holy Cross was a thing of the past. Feeling like a nomad, I carried my textbooks in a new red and blue "frosh bag" down the long corridors; I felt so insignificant, so puny, so immature.

The temporary recognition I had achieved as president of the eighth grade was now far behind me. My new environment served to amplify my basic feelings of inadequacy. On top of that, "Polack" jokes were the latest fad, and the void in my life—the hollowness—was surfacing once again. Desperately, I looked around for an outlet, something I could belong to.

"Orientation meeting for anyone interested in joining the 'Knights of the Altar' will be held in room 202 immediately following these announcements," came the raspy voice over the public address system.

By the second month at Saint Joe's, I became a Knight of the Altar, a sophisticated title for altar boy. It was something at which I had had some experience and was a good way to demonstrate my faith to my fellow students.

One day, after serving an early Mass in the school chapel, I grabbed my books, made the sign of the cross with holy water, genuflected, and headed for the cafeteria for some chocolate-covered doughnuts. As I went out the chapel door, I found myself directly behind three members of the football team. At the time, our team was undefeated and ranked as one of the best in the state, so it was a distinct privilege to be so close to them.

But as we moved along, I felt like a grape next to a trio of watermelons. I recognized one of the players from his picture in the paper—our six-foot-eight, two-hundred-eighty-five-pound tackle. Admiring his physique, I noticed how everyone in the congested corridors quickly moved aside so as not to obstruct his path.

Wow, I sighed to myself, everyone steps aside with such respect . . . that guy's biceps must be eighteen inches around! I wonder how long he works out each day? I'll just stick close behind him as we go through the cafeteria. Some of the guys may think I'm with him.

The more I gawked at the football players, the more I coveted what they represented. Then one day in study hall, I came across some previous Saint Joseph's yearbooks and noticed that many of my football idols were actually not much bigger as freshmen than I was.

If I started working out with weights right now, I said to myself, by the time I'm a junior, I could be as muscular as Dick Moore or Bill Vance or some of those other guys.

That void inside was going to be eradicated. I had the master plan that would bring me the satisfaction and importance I so thirsted for. Once again, I was going to be *somebody*.

I got a 220-pound set of weights (which was 120 pounds more than I could use) and began the "Bob Hoffman Body Building Course" in the secrecy of my bedroom. I pasted up pictures on my wall from the latest issues of *Mr. America*; mounted inspirational quotations like "When the going gets tough, the tough get going" on my mirror; and daily drank a quart of Bob Hoffman's special "Quick Weight-Gain Formula." I ate double portions at each meal and popped fifteen to thirty protein pills at various times throughout the day. Health foods—wheat germ, safflower seeds, and so on—became an integral part of my diet.

For six months I worked out an hour and a half every other day. Measuring my biceps, neck, chest, and legs at the start of my routine, I vowed that I would not stop until I had added at least two inches to each area. The schedule of exercises and the diet plan were intense, but I was determined to achieve my goals.

The countless hours of agonized straining seemed worth it when I heard a fellow changing clothes next to me in gym class say, "Hey, you been working out lately?"

It sounded so good, I wanted to hear it again. Slamming the locker door, I turned my head, saying, "Sorry, Tom, what'd you say?"

"I asked if you've been working out lately? You look like your arms are getting bigger."

Shrugging my shoulders, I replied, "Eh, off and on a bit."

Wow, it's starting to show! Throbbing with renewed determination, I jogged all the way home and immediately added five more repetitions to each exercise.

One day, late in my freshman year, I was going out the chapel door after serving Mass when I again encountered the three football players passing by the chapel. Still garbed in the ankle-length black cassock and slip-over white surplice, I ducked back inside.

Why did I do that? I asked myself. Why didn't I want them to see me?

Reflecting for a few seconds, I knew the answer: Football players didn't go for this sort of thing. They were rarely at Mass, let alone as a Knight of the Altar.

All of a sudden, that title, Knight of the Altar, sounded faintly repugnant to me. As I sat there quietly, some of the words of Mr. Straub, the gym instructor, came across my mind: "You're in high school now—you're not little babies anymore, with the Sisters around to wipe your nose." Other words began to permeate my thoughts: Guardian angel . . . rosary . . . Little Flower of Jesus . . . holy water . . . Blessed Virgin Mary—they all sounded so effeminate, so sissy.

I jumped slightly as the confessional door closed, and an elderly priest, Father Reich, came out and moved toward the chapel altar. Father Reich, for whom I had deep respect, was a frail priest about 5′8″, weighing little more than 120 pounds. As he went up to the altar, my eyes focused in on the white satin altar cloth. He picked up the floral bouquet that was on the altar and took it with him as he went out. Everything seemed so gentle, so delicate, so unmasculine.

Ring!
The bell for first period broke my thought pattern as I
darted out of the pew, hung up my server's outfit, and went to
my homeroom.

During the last week of school, I came to a decision. Having
re-evaluated the need to demonstrate my faith, I felt it best to
drop out of the Knights of the Altar entirely. Some strong
negative feelings were rapidly developing about being seen in
the chapel at all, so my visits became fewer and farther
between. I continued to go to Mass on Sunday at Holy Cross,
but the words "Holy Joe" kept surfacing in my mind. As my
freshman year came to an end, I found myself, for the first
time in my life, openly questioning my basic faith.

"The word sophomore means wise fool, and that's just what
most of you are." With that remark, Brother Fred Hiehle
welcomed our class back to school in September of 1964.

Having faithfully continued my body-building program over
the summer, I could tell the results were evident. A number of
my peers made favorable comments to me the first few weeks
back at Saint Joe's, and my ego blasted off into the glory of
each one.

"Hey, Mister Muscles, give me a hand with this desk."

"Larry, what size are your arms now?"

"You going to go out for football, Lar?"

Savoring my first real taste of admiration, I took out a
membership in a neighborhood work-out gym—"Raymond's
Athletic Club for the *Solid* Man." The environment and the
other weight lifters will be just the inspiration I need, I
thought.

But no sooner had I joined than a new star blazed into my
firmament—a constellation so bright that all else was soon
forgotten. One Sunday night about eight o'clock, my father
called to me from the living room.

"Larry, Larry! Hurry up. Come here." I put my homework

down on my desk and darted out of my bedroom. Dad was perched in front of the TV adjusting the picture as I entered the room.

"Man, I've got a load of homework to catch up on. What do you want?" I asked.

Dad didn't even turn to look at me, but kept moving the dials on the set. "Just watch," he said, "as soon as this commercial is over."

Hunkering down on my haunches, I focused my eyes on the screen. The commercial faded out, and then the familiar voice of Ed Sullivan proclaimed, "Ladies and gentlemen, let's all welcome to the United States—for their American debut—that *reealee* great group from England. Let's hear it for *The Beatles!*"

As the curtain opened, there, on the screen, appeared four mop-haired young men, attired in some very unique suits and wearing high-heeled boots. Three of them were playing guitars while one sat behind a set of drums shaking his head vigorously back and forth with the beat of the song, "I Want to Hold Your Hand." Their singing was barely audible amidst the perpetual screams of the audience. Punctuating every other line with a zesty "ow-ohh," the singers tossed their heads from side to side and tempestuously jerked their torsos to the driving rhythm of the music.

"How repulsive!" Mom asserted.

"Like a bunch of wild men!" Dad added.

"Cool," was all I could say. "Cool!"

As Mom and Dad expressed their outrage at the antics on the screen, I sat totally entranced by the "fab four." Thoughts began bouncing across my mental terrain— Look at the neat set of drums . . . and check that crazy clothing . . . Man, those chicks are going to *level* that stage; listen to those screams! Fantastic!

The next week at school, John, Paul, George, and Ringo

were the main subjects of everyone's conversation. And after the English rock group made two more successive appearances on the Ed Sullivan show, more than just the youth of the country was caught up in what the news media labeled as "Beatlemania." Within three short weeks, the Beatles—their music, hairstyle, and clothes—had hit the American scene like an earthquake.

A short time later, my four best friends from Holy Cross and Saint Joe's met with me in my basement to discuss an idea of momentous import. Ed called the meeting to order. "Let's get serious! Are we, or are we not, going to form a rock group?"

An affirmative response came immediately from each of us. There was only one problem: none of us played an instrument. Incredibly, at the time that seemed insignificant; all that mattered was that we had enough desire to see the idea materialize. Fortunately there was no one there to show us how impossible the idea was.

So it was decided. We were to enroll in Sodja's Music Studio and begin music lessons, each one on his respective instrument. I would be on drums, Ed Gozoski on lead guitar, Denny Carleton on rhythm guitar, Chuck McKinley on bass, and Rich Schonauer on sax. The name of the group? We would call ourselves "The Lost Souls."

Any further weight lifting aspirations would have to wait. After all, how often did one have the prospect of being part of a famous rock group? Concert appearances before thousands of adoring fans . . . hit records . . . million-seller albums . . . cross-country tours . . . newspaper and magazine articles . . . expensive wardrobes . . . money . . . fame—all that flashed before my mind's eye.

Larry, I said to myself, you're going to be somebody! You're going to be a V.I.P., a rock star. So long, emptiness. Larry Tomczak is going to make it big!

And so, for the next five months, each of us studied music; it was tedious, and our progress seemed unbearably slow, but none of us lost sight of our goal, though it took constant mutual encouragement.

Finally, we purchased our instruments and began practicing as a group. Two or three days a week for a minimum of three hours, The Lost Souls practiced. This, of course, was in addition to our solo practice.

Withdrawing my entire life savings of nine hundred and three dollars, I had purchased one of the finest sets of drums on the market. My new, gray-ripple, dual-tom, dual-cymbal set of Rogers drums was to be my key to prosperity. Mom and Dad were bitterly antagonistic, to put it mildly.

"Larry! Stop that stupid pounding!" my mother would holler down to the basement where I was furiously building a tempo. Sitting next to me was my portable record player with the volume on max. "Satisfaction" by the Rolling Stones or "Light My Fire" by the Doors were usually the discs spinning on the turntable.

Again the voice would come. "I *said*, stop that pounding! Listen here, young man, you're to obey when I tell you to do something. As long as you're in *my* house, you'll do as I say. If you don't like it, there's the door!"

Infuriated by the interruption, I'd re-grip my sticks and commence to play with even more vehemence.

The scream from upstairs would pierce like a siren: "*Larry! I can't stand it anymore! Stop it, or I'll smash those drums! Stop it!*"

As my arteries exploded, I would slam down my drumsticks or fling them at the concrete wall, clench my fists, jump off my seat, and fly into a rage. The basement door would slam shut, and I'd pace the floor saying, just loud enough *not* to be heard upstairs, "Go to hell! I wish you were back in that stupid hospital!"

Mom had stayed in the hospital six months for her hip surgery and therapy, and though I sympathized with her, I could not permit her or anyone else to suppress my ambitions. After all, I thought, I've got a future to be concerned about. They just don't understand, that's all.

And so tension mounted in our family. Margaret, who was away most of the time in beauticians' school, rarely got involved in any of the altercations. When she was home, I could usually count on her support, in the form of an oft-repeated statement—"Aw, Mom-and-Dad, don't be so old-fashioned."

Being in a rock group was not exactly what my parents had envisioned for my life. Having a rock drummer for a son just didn't fit the Polish Catholic mold. An engineer, a lawyer, a teacher, anything—even a shoemaker or butcher—but not a hippie rock star. I was well aware of this and oftentimes found myself gloating over the fact that it bothered them. I would make it big in spite of all the obstacles they'd placed in my path.

My junior year at Saint Joseph's revolved around the band. Our group started out performing at a few backyard parties and then in a series of CYO parish dances in Euclid. Our band personality and overall image more than compensated for our musical handicaps. The Lost Souls had a large following of nubile young girls whose presence at a dance insured a throng of eager young guys. Our bookings soon included the area high school mixers, and when it came time for our debut at Saint Joe's, our band broke all attendance records with a crowd of eleven hundred young people. We were starting to go places—fast!

My need to be somebody was slowly but surely being satisfied. My ego was continually shooting up, while the void seemed to be steadily diminishing. Being in the band meant being on a stage—with hundreds of adulating eyes looking up to me. Lining up the best-looking girls was now a piece of cake, in fact, they practically had to wait their turn. Money was no problem, either; thirty bucks a night for three hours' work was our usual take per man. It was also quite an ego-fix to walk into McDonalds' and have someone whisper as I passed by, "Hey, that's one of The Lost Souls."

The Mr. America photographs and inspirational clichés had long been removed from my small wood-paneled bedroom. And since my room was my one private enclave, it was adorned to reflect my world. To my parents, it was a fool's paradise: posters of rock idols, band photographs, stacks of albums, peace-symbol medallions. To me, it was where I was at, and where I was going. Once the door was closed, the amphitheater and its cast came alive. Larry Tomczak was the star célèbre, and the main spotlight was ever so warm. The stillness of the crowd was assurance of an attentive and appreciative audience. The music from my record player began, "C'mon baby, light my fire . . ."

And so, eyes closed and lips syncopating the lyrics, I would trip out into my world. It was so easy to visualize The Lost Souls stepping onto a really big stage before thousands of expectant fans.

On my left wall was a poster of the finest guitarist and showman I had ever seen—Jimi Hendrix. Garbed in a slippery black costume, his hand poised like a claw to pounce his guitar, his legs wide apart, his face in an agony of travail, Jimi stood transfixed before his massive amplifier. A bold caption was emblazoned across the base of the poster: "I CHEW ALUMINUM FOIL."

Dead-center in my middle wall was a poignant poster enshrining the patron saint of my rock world. Attired in skin-tight black leather pants, Jim Morrison of the Doors stood majestically draped over a microphone. Yellow and red flames crawled up his legs while the smoke formed letters above his head, "LIGHT MY FIRE."

A third poster was of the progenitors of it all, the Beatles. John Lennon, Paul McCartney, George Harrison, and Ringo

Starr—they seemed immortal, superhuman, beyond description.

I got my hair cut in a shag, bought some wire-rimmed sunglasses, and searched in every "mod" clothing store in Cleveland for a pair of leather pants.

I bought all the albums released by my gods. My bedroom floor was stacked with them. Such incongruous titles as "Magical Mystery Tour," "Strange Days," and "Their Satanic Majesties Request" headed up my collection of "heavies," and many of the album songs were performed regularly by The Lost Souls.

It was always a lift to go into my room after school, shut the door, put the latest Stones album on the record player full blast, fall back on the bed, and absorb myself into the sounds.

"Larry! *Larry!* Do you have to play that *noise* so loud?" Mom would call out from the kitchen.

"You can't feel it unless it's loud," I'd shout back. "I've got to hear the drums, and I can't pick them out unless the volume is up."

"Well as long as you're in my house, *turn it down!*"

Jumping from the bed, I'd utter a stream of obscenities while lowering the volume.

I went to see my gods whenever they came to Cleveland. During the final month of my junior year in high school, Jim Morrison and the Doors came to Cleveland's Public Hall for a one-night concert. I was one of the fortunate ones who had purchased a ticket months in advance. As the police prepared to open the gates to ten thousand young people, one very excited, sixteen-year-old drummer could be seen inches from the entrance.

From my balcony seat, I peered out over the cavernous auditorium; the thousands of people milling about the ground floor made a weird kaleidoscope.

The usual technical difficulties delayed the show, and the

audience was extremely restless. The atmosphere was pregnant with expectancy, and marijuana smoke began permeating the air. Two solid rows of blue-uniformed police stood elbow to elbow at the front of the stage, where the Door's equipment—six oversize, high-wattage amplifiers, a Hammond organ, and a set of drums—stood ready to discharge their rhythmic pulsations. Rhythmic handclapping in the rear balcony began to reverberate throughout Public Hall as a chain response grew.

"Now! Now! Now! Now! Now!" the foot-stomping crowd clamored. The Roman Colosseum had been resurrected. With each word, the youthful audience leaned forward more and more as the catapult readied. Then, just at the maximum moment, the public address system beckoned—*"Ladies and gentlemen, let's welcome the Doors!"*

There was a deafening cheer, the velvet curtains parted, and out ran the four members of the Doors. My eyes immediately focused on the man in the black leather skin-tight outfit, with the shoulder-length tousled hair and the unshaven face. It was the man on my poster, the Olympian, Jim Morrison.

Tuning out everything else in the auditorium, I sat under the spell of his awesome presence for over forty minutes. Even his mile-high condition could not deter my enthusiasm, as he sang song after song from his albums.

Closing my eyes for a few seconds between numbers, I repeated under my breath, "You've got to do it. . . . You've *got* to do 'Light My Fire.' "

Suddenly the organ released the chord I had been waiting for.

"That's it!" I shouted. "Light My Fire!" And pandemonium broke loose.

I joined with the audience in springing to my feet. Drumming the beat ferociously on the seat in front of me with my hands, I let my eyes sweep over the multitude below. Hands were clapping, heads were bobbing, and a swarm of young people were leaving their seats to besiege the stage. In seconds, the momentum peaked as the small army of frenzied youth became a deluge of mobbing, pushing, shoving, incalculable masses. All of a sudden, a young girl next to me shouted, "Oh my God, look at the stage!"

Hundreds of riot-torn police had formed a human wall to protect themselves and the musicians from the advancing stampede. Using their nightsticks and feet, the officers clubbed and kicked for their lives, and blood was oozing from the heads of a number in the vanguard of the melee. As the band members quickly darted off-stage, the house lights came on, and a voice over the public address system announced that the concert was over. The riot fizzled as fast as it started. Sweating profusely and coughing from the stuffy air, the crowd began to disperse. As thousands left Public Hall, one word of reaction repeatedly punctuated the late evening conversations: "Cool!"

In 1966, as a senior at Saint Joe's, my life-style was an extension of the previous year. The Lost Souls had top priority, and the group was now being paid top dollar for every concert. By midyear, we were members of the Cleveland Musicians' Union. We hired an equipment manager to transport our $5,000 worth of equipment in our newly purchased Chevy van.

Playing engagements in other states and plans for our first record all combined to bring the realization of my dreams within reach. The Lost Souls were doing more original numbers, and with each engagement, we were sounding and looking more professional, with all the accouterments, especially long hair.

In the mid-sixties, our hair length brought us ridicule and harrassment wherever we went. But there was one place where the derogatory remarks seemed the most incisive—Holy Cross Church.

All five of us had been raised in Holy Cross parish, and we

did almost everything together, including attendance at Sunday Mass. Yet this duty was becoming increasingly loathsome. Even attending the extra-early service in the basement of the church, we could not avoid "remarks."

Shrieking sirens and a flashing neon sign might just as well have gone into operation the moment we started down that aisle.

"Isn't that disgusting!" an elderly woman whispered from inside one of the rows on our left.

"That little blond looks like a girl," stage-whispered a male seated to the right.

"Bunch of queers, that's what they are!"

"*Shhh*—not so loud, honey."

Finding our row, we murmured, "Excuse us," to the man sitting in the end row seat. Making obvious his displeasure at being disturbed, he slowly rose to let us pass.

"Ouch!"

Oh, wow! I had stepped on his shoe. I forced a smile and stated my apology.

"Too important to watch where you're going?" he challenged.

"Sorry."

"You should be!"

Once we were in our seats, all of us were safe—for forty-five minutes until the end of Mass. Because returning from the communion rail was too much like a "fashion show," we had long since agreed that it was best to by-pass Communion and remain in the security of our seats.

When Mass ended, the congregation began the mass exodus. Shuffling along with the slow movement of the crowd, we heard the abrasive comments resume, more direct.

"Excuse me," said a middle-aged man who was walking beside his wife and three children, "but don't you think you people are a little disrespectful?"

Experience had taught us not to reply, no matter how we

were provoked. I smiled and ignored the remark. The hallway to the outdoor parking lot was only twenty feet away.

"Want to borrow a couple of bucks for a haircut?"

"I thought girls always wore dresses to church, didn't you, honey?"

Ten more feet.

"Hey, do you young ladies know where the restroom is?"

Looking neither to the right or left, we walked through the hallway, up the steps, out the doors, and straight to the car.

Piling into Ed Gozoski's shiny red two-year-old Catalina, which we had nicknamed the Gozmobile, we slammed the door—and exploded.

"Those rotten, lousy hypocrites!"

"I'd like to take on that big-mouthed one who called us queers. I could deck him in about ten seconds!"

"Yeah, and then throw him on top of that tub-bellied usher!"

"What a bunch of phonies! Makes you want to puke in the collection basket!"

"Don't bother picking me up for Mass next week—I've had it with Holy Cross!"

"I'll pick you up in my dad's car, and we can drive around for the hour, okay?"

"Yeah, I better; I don't want to get in another go-around with my dad about Mass. Man, I can't wait till I go to college next year and won't have to put up with his forcing me to go."

So, some of The Lost Souls joined the rapidly growing sector of seniors from Saint Joseph's who had long since ceased attending Mass.

The final straw came after an interview and picture of Denny Carleton, our rhythm guitarist, in the Cleveland *Plain Dealer*. Each one of us received a special delivery telegram from Saint Joseph's principal that stated, in effect: "Get a haircut or get out of school!"

Immediately we set up an appointment with our principal.

"All right, what is it you fellows want to see me about?" he asked, when we were admitted into his office.

I assumed the role of spokesman and replied, "Well, it's about the tele—"

"There's nothing to talk about!" he exclaimed. "I told you to get a haircut. If you refuse to comply, well, then I'm afraid I'll have no recourse but to expel you."

Chuck dropped all pretense of diplomacy. "Now why-the-heck does my hair length make any difference to you?"

"Listen, Mister McKinley, don't you get smart with me! This school has a reputation to maintain in the Cleveland community. When a picture appears in our state's largest newspaper protraying Mr. Carleton over there looking like a girl and then 'proudly' proclaiming himself to be a 'Saint Joseph's Viking,' that's going too far!"

"But I keep my hair neat and clean," Denny interjected.

"That's not the issue."

"Then what *is?*"

The principal stood up. "We have rules, and you are going to abide by them. When you graduate from this school, you can paint yourself blue and run naked in Municipal Stadium for all I care, but until that time, the operative word is going to be obedience. Is that understood?"

Our principal had spoken. It was obvious that begging and pleading would get us nowhere. So we got our haircuts but nurtured growing enmity in our hearts toward our principal and everything he stood for. And that included the Roman Catholic church.

It had not happened overnight; the snowball had been rolling downhill for a long time. The blind dutiful obedience of grade school had long since changed into apathy, and was rapidly hardening into contempt. The ridicule we received at Mass and the apparent hypocrisy in our instruction were our ostensible motives for tuning off the Church, but in actuality, neither pinpointed the real, deep-seated cause. There were too many other young people who were *not* being subjected to ridicule or any kind of "ultimatum" and who were part of the swelling exodus. Of my eleven closest friends, all Catholics, nine had already withdrawn from the Church. Something else was wrong. Something that precipitated a remark frequently heard from both youth and adults—"Let's go to an early Mass Sunday and get it over with."

"Have a seat, Larry. Make yourself comfortable," the priest said.

Sitting down in the old leather chair he indicated, I found myself face to face with Father Ken Sommer, the chaplain of Saint Joseph's. Now in his late thirties, his close-cropped hair was turning gray, but he still maintained much of the physique he had developed as an All-American football player for Dayton University. His genuine interest in each guy who came to him and his real compassion made Father Sommer about the most popular faculty member at our high school.

It was May of 1967, two weeks before graduation. My turn had come for a final counseling session in Father Sommer's familiar little office. Not much bigger than two telephone booths, the cubicle was conducive to the kind of informal "rap" sessions that Father Ken preferred.

"You know, I think you're going to make it! Congratulations!"

"Thanks, Father. It's kind of hard to believe," I replied.

"Well, Larry, we've got about fifteen minutes; how do you want to use it? I'm here to listen."

"All right. Would you like to hear some honest complaints?"

"Go right ahead. I just hope they're not all about me!"

Both of us laughed, and I began.

"Yesterday, for some reason, I couldn't help but think about the years I've spent in school. Twelve years is a long time. I

wonder if it was really worth it for my parents to work so
darned hard to send me to Catholic school, when I could have
gone to a public school for free."

Father Sommer leaned forward in his swivel chair, cupped
his hands together, and encouraged me with a nod.

"Father, I've got to level with you. I resent having been
indoctrinated into a Church that seems so hypocritical and
shallow—and, frankly, meaningless." I paused for him to
register shock, but he just kept looking at me intently. So I
went on.

"Look around at the guys in this school, Father. We all
came here from our little parochial schools, having naïvely and
fearfully accepted everything the Sisters taught us. Then, all
the freshman year, we were told that we weren't kids
anymore—no one was going to hold our hand or wipe our
nose. We were told to start thinking for ourselves." I slapped
the arm of my chair.

"And so we started doing just that, asking questions and
looking for reality, not fantasy. But as soon as we'd ask a
question about something in the Catholic Church, we were
given the fast runaround. 'Because the Church *says* so, that's
why!' Father, have you any idea how many kids in this school
are either atheists or agnostics and how many could care less
about going to Mass?"

Father Sommer looked me in the eye and spoke without
smiling. "I think I do, Larry. I've talked to enough of the group
to know what you're saying is true. I also know that hundreds
of you guys are getting bombed on weekends, and a few of you
are beginning to mess around with marijuana, because you're
searching for peace and purpose in life, and you're not finding
them in the Church, so you're looking in the world." He
paused. "Larry, have you given up on the Church, too?"

"Father, you know Mom and Dad. If I dropped out of the
Church now, I'd break their hearts. And I couldn't live with
myself if I did that. So I go to Mass with them, and I guess I'll

just go on playing church like so many people do. An hour at Mass on Sunday won't kill me, huh?"

Father Sommer looked at me and shook his head. "No, it won't kill you, Larry."

I was about to stand up to say goodbye when out of nowhere the oddest thought popped into my mind. It was a question I had often contemplated long ago, especially while sitting bored in church.

"Father," I said, "there's one thing I can't figure out."

"Only one?" he smiled.

"Well, if it's so obvious that the Church is dying fast, how come God doesn't do a miracle or two to shake things up?"

Father Sommer looked at me with a startled expression on his face. "That's really strange. I was asking myself that same question a month ago. But do you know, I just may have seen what might be part of the answer?"

He leaned forward, more animated than at any time in our meeting. "A few weeks ago, I had a call from an attorney friend of mine, who asked me to go with him for a prayer meeting at Notre Dame University. I had no idea what was in store, but I had a strong leading to go.

"We got to Notre Dame about 10:30 at night and went to a small room where about thirty people, mostly Catholics, were praying—out loud. Many had their hands uplifted; they were singing, reading the Bible, and talking about what Jesus Christ had been doing in their lives and how they had found peace and new life. They prayed so deeply and yet openly that it was almost as if the Lord was right there in the room with them!"

He stopped for a moment and seemed to be weighing whether to go on. Apparently he got a green light. "Larry, do you remember what happened on Pentecost?"

"Uh, yeah, I think so," I said. "Wasn't that when there was an outpouring of the Holy Spirit on the disciples and some of the other believers?"

"That's right! What else happened?"

I thought for a moment. "They began to speak in other tongues, didn't they?"

Father Sommer bolted up from his chair. "What would you say if I told you that the same thing is going on today, right *now* in the Catholic Church? I saw it at Notre Dame!"

I got up, shook his hand, and got out of there as fast as I could.

Man, the pressure's gotten too much for him, I thought, as I hurried down the empty corridor. He's starting to flip out.

But something he said earlier, I could not get out of my mind. "You're searching for peace and purpose in life and you're not finding them in the Church, so you're looking in the world."

4

SEX!
Now that we've got your attention, take
a form and step in line.

"Hey, that's a pretty clever sign," I said to Chuck, as we approached the registration tables.

"Yeah, I guess college kids are a little more ingenious than high schoolers."

Nodding, I picked up my three-page form from one of the folding tables lined up along the walls of the auditorium and proceeded to step into the line "T through Z." It was September 29, 1967, Freshman Registration Day at CSU, and the atmosphere was like a giant overcrowded supermarket on Saturday morning.

How are they ever going to handle two thousand freshmen registrations? I wondered, as I counted the heads in front of me, all forty-six of them. And I thought Saint Joe's was crowded!

As I surveyed the mobs of young people, the old feelings of insecurity began to surface. Everywhere I looked, there were people, walking . . . standing . . . talking . . . waiting . . . short and tall and pretty and homely and black and white and long-haired and short-haired. Some of the girls were in skirts, but many joined the guys in tie-dyed blue jeans or shorts.

Reaching for the pencil that I had stuck over my ear, I

began to fill out the form. With each completed line, I felt increasingly more insignificant.

Address, 310 East 200th Street; zip code, 44119; phone number, 216-531-0808; social security number, 283-44-4589; student identification number, D561832967; license plate number, AJ4609. Man, talk about anonymity!

Being a commuter school, CSU lacked a natural campus environment. Compacted into an area taking up scarcely two city blocks, the campus's telephone poles, parking meters, and concrete sidewalks substituted for the traditional lawns and shady oak trees.

And to think I felt lost my first day at Saint Joe's, I thought. This is going to be a whole new world!

And it was.

My first few months as a freshman in college were discouraging—as I put it, "a real waste." The prerequisite courses that I was forced to take, the aloofness of the instructors, and the complexity of the textbook material combined to make me dislike college life intensely. Not surprisingly, my first-quarter grades reflected my attitude; three C's and a D were the best I could achieve. I wanted out, but something was holding me back.

Hell, no—we won't go! The anti-Vietnam demonstrations at CSU were a constant reminder to me why I should *not* withdraw from college. As long as I stayed in school, I could not be drafted. In addition, there was a monthly letter from Mike Jolly, a close friend stationed in Saigon. His descriptions of the atrocities of the war on both sides further strengthened my conviction.

But even though college was a drag, there was still the band and the world of rock music. After practicing four or five days each week all summer long, The Lost Souls cut their first record. The expense was phenomenal, but now that we were "professional" recording artists, monetary affairs could no longer be of any concern. The addition of a new lead guitarist,

Den Marek, to replace Ed Gozoski was the only change in the group. Den, who had seven years more experience on guitar, gave the band what we felt was an even fuller sound. We were on our way to the big time, and nothing was going to stand in our way.

And one day, the icing was indeed put on our cake. Midway through my freshman year, The Lost Souls secured an engagement for an open-air concert in the eighty-thousand-seat Cleveland Municipal Stadium. It all seemed absolutely unreal—The Lost Souls performing a concert in one of the three largest stadiums in the United States.

Standing inside the home-team dugout with my right foot on the first step, I ran my fingers again through my freshly washed hair. The other Lost Souls were posed in similar positions along the base of the dugout, each one absorbing the immensity of the moment. Our new London-tailored, pin-striped suit-coats looked so expensive, so professional—so "cool." Admiring them, I suddenly had a wild thought and broke up.

"What's the matter?" Denny Carleton shouted.

"Nothing. I just thought what a fantastic scene it would be if we painted ourselves blue and ran out there naked!"

Denny stared at me like I'd fallen out of my tree and then remembered and collapsed with laughter, along with the other, older, Lost Souls.

Thousands of young people occupying the upper and lower deck seats in the Municipal Stadium were impatiently clapping their hands as our equipment managers hurried to make the final technical adjustments on our stage equipment. The raised wooden stage was situated directly over second base on the playing field.

That's the exact spot where the Beatles performed, I thought. Imagine, the last group to use that stage was the Beatles—now it's The Lost Souls.

The handclapping grew louder, and the electric tension started to build. Now it was *our* group performing. The Lost

Souls were in the spotlight, and Larry Tomczak was the drummer.

"You guys ready?"

"Ready!" two or three of us responded in jagged unison. Denny and Rich both pulled away from the water cooler as Chuck and Den picked up the guitars.

Instantly, the public address system of the stadium echoed, *"Ladies and gentlemen, let's welcome The Lost Souls!"*

Springing from the dugout, the five of us darted across the playing field toward the stage. The thunderous reception was deafening; the exaltation made every single minute of practice worthwhile.

"Oh God, don't let me trip," I pleaded as I approached the stage.

Taking the steps two at a time, I stopped the moment my feet were firmly on the platform. In nonchalant fashion, I sauntered across the stage to my drums, grabbed my set of drumsticks, and sat down, poised for action. Lifting my eyes to the crowd for the first time, I felt a wild chill shoot through my body. Every fantasy I had ever had was realized in that instant. And it was better—it was real. In supreme ecstasy, I sat on my percussion throne, and knew that every eye in Cleveland Stadium was focused on me.

For the next twenty-five minutes, I was in bliss. As the electric guitars vibrated the powerful amplifiers, I helped to build each crescendo with rolling explosions of drum bursts and crashing cymbals. Caught in the spell of raw, base emotion unleashed and translated to the semblance of a melodic line, the youthful audience began to sway with the rhythm and lose themselves increasingly in each song. Some were completely gone, possessed, dancing on their seats or in the aisles, jerking insanely to the frenzy of the electrically charged sounds. And I was the dance-master, the drumstick my baton. So this was power . . .

"Larry? Hey, Larry!" Denny shouted over, as he turned the volume on his amp still higher.

"Huh? What is it?"

"Do 'Nights in White Satin' next."

"But isn't that our last number?" I asked.

"Yeah, twenty-minute concert, that's all we're allowed, and we're over that already," Denny said, as he hurried back to his microphone.

"Oh, wow!" I said, swearing and taking it out on the drums. "We only just got started!"

As our last song drew to a close, I sensed my heartbeat slowly sinking deeper into melancholy with each diminishing beat.

In less than five minutes, I found myself sitting on a splintered bench in a makeshift dressing room. Outside the well-guarded door to my left, I could hear the rustling movement of hundreds of young female fans awaiting our exit. Having loosened my tie, I sat perfectly still and stared at the floor where a fly was crawling over a lump of dried mud. It's over, I thought. The whole thing is over. And we only just got started . . .

In less than a year, The Lost Souls band was no more. When it happened, I simply could not believe it. My senses seemed disconnected, the malaise affecting my body was so intense that even my breathing was impaired.

How could we all just abandon everything? I thought. The thousands of practice hours, the thousands of dollars invested in our instruments and the amps and the van, the hundreds of promotional pictures, the record, all the clothing . . . the money . . . the recognition . . .

The debacle of The Lost Souls was not the result of one altercation. Numerous problems had been snowballing for months. The record had failed to galvanize the area promoters.

Waning interest in taking the music seriously combined with a contented complacency with the progress in the group. And personality clashes had become bitter and frequent. When Denny Carleton announced that he was quitting, the inscription on the tombstone was clear.

"Well," I said with a sigh, "it had to happen sooner or later." But I was unable to repress the surge of grief welling up in my heart. Once back in my room, I closed my eyes and surrendered to tears.

The spotlight had gone out. My dream had been perforated, torn and neatly discarded before my very eyes.

Boozing it up on weekends became a regular activity for me in my sophomore year at CSU. Buying a couple of six-packs and a bag of chips and then driving to a secluded parking lot with a girl was my primary form of amusement.

Beer provided escape from the void which had grown larger than ever; the trouble was, it never lasted long enough. Every Saturday morning after a drinking spree, I still had to face myself in the mirror as I came back to reality. And each time it got worse.

My aversion toward college life remained unchanged. Now that band practices were over, I found myself almost forced to use some of the time on studies. I needed to declare a major field of study, and I had absolutely no idea what I wanted to do.

"So what are you going to do with your life, Larry?" came the dreaded question from my parents, relatives, neighbors, and vocational counselor. And I had no answer.

On New Year's Day, 1969, our family invited our immediate relatives over for a holiday social. Our Christmas decorations were still in place, and a festive spirit pervaded the afternoon. The dining-room table was covered with a sumptuous spread of cold cuts, piping hot baked beans, Polish *Kielbasa*, and a tantalizing variety of homemade cookies, as our relatives were encouraged by Mom to "fill up those plates."

With a drink in one hand and an overfilled paper plate in the other, my cousins, aunts, and uncles moved away from the buffet into the living room. I sat on the couch, flipping through a stack of Christmas cards.

"So what are you going to do with your life, Larry?" asked Uncle Bob.

Opening my mouth to put forth my standard reply, I was interrupted.

"Why don't you go into metallurgy!" Uncle Ken interjected.

"No," Aunt Irene asserted, "he's more the type for a social worker or a teacher."

Still chewing on a piece of homemade *kuchen*, Uncle Tom didn't wait to swallow. "There's no money in those professions for a man. He should go on to law school and become an attorney."

Mom, who was making the rounds with a pot of coffee, suddenly turned and waved her forefinger at me. "You'd just better make up your mind—*quick!*"

"Look!" I exploded. "I don't know what I want to do! Now will you just get off my back, for crying out loud!"

Throwing the stack of Christmas cards on the floor, I stood up, strode across the room, and slammed into my bedroom. No one uttered a sound. My bedroom, long since stripped of its psychedelic ornamentation, was still my place of refuge. Looking in the mirror for the first real time, I asked, "Who am I? Where did I come from? Where *am* I going?" Nobody answered.

Frustration and tension were building in our home. My parents, who seemed to badger me constantly about every-thing, were prime targets for my outbursts. In our arguments, their age (both were now sixty) and lack of education made

them appear to me hopelessly out of touch with reality. I
gloated over the fact that much of my college vocabulary was
beyond their comprehension and deliberately injected words
like "acrimonious" and "obtuse" into our more heated arguments to rub their noses in how ignorant they were. Their
response was almost always the same—

*"Listen, young man. As long as you're in our house, you'll
do as we say! If you don't like it–there's the door!"*

There was also trouble with my sister, Margaret, who was
now twenty-one years old. A year ago, she had been dating a
six-foot-eight, two-hundred-ninety-pound football player from
Villanova University—the same tackle that I had idolized at
Saint Joe's—who had just been picked as the first draft choice
of one of the strongest teams in the NFL.

Margaret had been happily making plans for a wedding, but
one day, after four years of going steady, the football hero
notified her that it was all over.

My sister went into a state of shock. Her whole world caved
in; all vanished in a puff of smoke. The hurt and resultant
bitterness and hostility could be stuffed down only so long. So
Margaret took it out on the family, while at the same time
deadening the pain through alcohol.

One night the uproar was worse than usual. Turning over in
bed, I pulled the pillow over my head to muffle the shouting.
The luminous hands on my watch pointed to three-thirty.
Gritting my teeth, I finally blew up. "Will you people shut
your damn mouths!"

I sprang out of bed, flung open my door, and stormed to the
kitchen with my fists clenched.

"Margaret," Mom was pleading, "you've got to stop ruining
your life! Nursing that grudge, keeping it alive—it's going to
destroy you. Can't you see that?"

Mom was in her pajamas and slippers, kneeling on the
kitchen floor. Her hands were cupped around the face of my

sister who was on the floor, propped up against the stove in a stupor.

Tears were running down Mom's cheeks as she slid her hands down to Margaret's shoulders and tried to shake her back into reality.

"Margaret . . . Margaret, honey . . . listen to me."

Slowly my sister raised her eyelids. Squinting, shoving Mom's hands away, she spat out, "Shut up! Leave me alone! I'll do as I damned please with my life!"

Mother slapped her face. "Don't you talk to me that way, young lady!"

Margaret stumbled to her feet. "If I want to ruin my life, that's *my* business, see?"

Mother sobbed uncontrollably, and Dad, furious at being awakened, burst from his room.

"I'm not putting up with this any longer! I've got to get some sleep; I have to get up at 5:30 while Margaret sleeps it off till noon! I hope the police nab you driving drunk. Then they'll throw you in jail where you belong!"

Margaret staggered out of the kitchen, passing me without seeing me, and tottered up the bedroom stairs.

Bang! Her door slammed, and the episode was over—for that night.

All of us tried to help Margaret, but she had built such a shell around herself that there didn't seem to be any way through it.

For the past half a year, she had been downing more than a dozen drinks a night, five or six nights a week, in bar after bar. A sloe-gin fizz or a rum and coke were her only companions.

Margaret was smoking two packs of cigarettes a day, her language was becoming steadily coarser, and having lost her job, she collected unemployment compensation while sleeping till after noon every day. She didn't even look like herself; in less than a year she had gained sixty-five pounds.

Our home was hell. The surging undercurrent of raw hatred and mistrust was growing stronger every day, like gangrene, corrupting each one of us. Now we were at each other's throats all the time—except for one hour on Sunday when the Tomczaks "worshiped together as a family."

Mass . . . No sooner were we in the pew than I let my mind wander where it pleased: I hope we get one of the younger priests today; they always get it over with faster. . . . We've been going to Sunday Mass together for so long that if we ever stopped, we wouldn't know what to do with ourselves. . . . I wonder how many people would bother coming to Mass if all of a sudden the Pope announced it would be a "voluntary" obligation? I bet three-fourths of the people would disappear in a month's time, maybe more. . . . Look at those empty front pews. Hmmm, they should put some foam-rubber cushions in those first three rows; then it wouldn't look so bad. . . . Oh brother, what a sermon! He could play a tape recorder up there, and nobody'd notice. . . . Uh oh, time for the collection. Look at all the nickels in that basket. I bet if it weren't for parking meters and church collection baskets, the government could do away with nickels! . . . I'm glad I hardly ever see any college kids at Mass; this way, no one sees me, either. . . . Good, it's communion time. I hope there's a good fashion show today. . . . Man alive, dig all the people cutting out of church early; wonder if there will be enough left to sing the closing hymn. . . .

At last, like a long-awaited finale to a well-worn film, Father extended his hands for the benediction: "Go in peace, the Mass has ended."

The echoed response from the congregation followed: "Thanks be to God."

Yeah, I said to myself, Thanks be to God!

Junior year began in September of 1969, and I had picked Communications as my major. I began to buckle down to my studies, but good grades, I discovered, were hard work, a lot harder than I was used to.

One afternoon, while I was reading the newspaper, an advertisement caught my eye: "Read three to five times faster, comprehend more, improve your reading ability, all in *just* eight short weeks. Enroll today!"

And so I enrolled in a Cleveland speed-reading institute at a cost of one hundred and fifty dollars, and every Saturday morning I spent three hours in a classroom, developing the skill.

Because I was devoting so much time to reading and study each day, it was not long before I went to an eye doctor for my first pair of glasses.

One of the books I read, *How to Win Friends and Influence People* by Dale Carnegie, contained subject matter that was irresistible to me: Six Ways to Make People Like You; Twelve Ways to Win People to Your Way of Thinking; Fundamental Techniques in Handling People; Nine Ways to Change People . . .

"Wow!" I sighed, the night I completed the last chapter. "If I can keep advancing intellectually and master these techniques, I will make it big for sure! People will look up to me. I can start gaining friendships and establishing contacts that will really pay off someday."

Seated comfortably in a smooth black leather chair in the cubicle law office that a friend's father, who was an attorney, let me use, I leaned back and put my feet up on the desk. The wood-paneled interior of the attorney's office, decorated with numerous impressive plaques and certificates, encompassed me in stately security.

Although I was not a smoker, something compelled me to take a cigarette from the gold cigarette box on the desk. Lighting up, I exhaled and followed the smoke as it ascended to the ceiling. One of the overhead fluorescent lamps was flickering; it was almost burned out.

Noticing how rapidly the puff of smoke dissolved, and that the lamp was about to black out, I began to think about my own life.

Where would I really be, five, ten, twenty-five years from now? Would I be struggling for survival like that lamp? Like Dad still had to struggle? Or would I be like the smoke—gone?

The instant I posed the last question, I felt extremely discomfited. Immediately I took my feet off the desk, straightened up in the chair, and picked up the Dale Carnegie book again to avoid any further thinking. Death was a subject I chose to avoid. There was enough time to think about it later.

Setting my eyes on the last page, I started to read—

"If you have enjoyed this book, then you might be interested in checking your local directory for the 'Dale Carnegie Leadership Course' conducted in your city."

Hey! I said to myself, maybe they have one of these courses in Cleveland.

Pulling out the phone book, I was elated to find a listing for the "Dale Carnegie Course" in the downtown Statler-Hilton Hotel.

It took less than a week for me to register in the "Dale Carnegie Course in Effective Speaking and Human Relations." The $225 registration fee just about wiped out my savings account, but I was certain my training would pay off a hundredfold.

My class met one evening a week for four hours, which meant that my schedule would be more hectic than ever, and reading and speaking assignments would consume even more time. Yet I was determined to see it through. Rubbing shoulders with people in high-salaried executive and managerial positions was certain to pay off. The more contact I had with success-oriented people and techniques, the more ambitious I would become.

One day while speeding home from school on the freeway, an idea hit me like a thunderbolt.

Why not put some of my human relations training and intelligence to good use right now! Fourteen thousand students at the university need a leader—a dynamic, perceptive, and aggressive leader. Why not get involved—get my name known—and then next year I could be president of the student body! Think of it—the power, the status, friends, recognition . . .

The idea was *perfect*. But I knew that it would require immediate action and phenomenal perseverance. It would mean sacrificing sleep, girls, and maybe even food. But in the end, the benefits would far outweigh the effort.

The very next day I joined the CSU student government. Feigning genuine interest wherever I went, I immersed myself in every possible activity on campus—Marketing Club, Management Club, Environmental Affairs, International Students Alliance, Student Government Committees, and many others.

My schedule was becoming unbelievable, yet each day I was making more contacts with students, all of whom I regarded as potential voters. I carried a full, sixteen-hour-a-week academic load; one evening a week I attended the Dale Carnegie Course; Saturday morning was spent at the speed-reading school; forty hours a week I worked in an office of a local corporation; faster and faster I was reading more and more books, magazines, and newspapers; and, having attained straight A's for the first time in my life, I was determined to repeat the performance.

To avoid the tension and hostile atmosphere of home, I spent all my evenings in the law office, reading and studying.

Naturally, my academic success went right to my head, and I began to fancy myself in a new role—that of an intellectual. Engaging in discussions that demonstrated my mental prowess was a most gratifying pastime, particularly with my less learned friends and relatives.

"Well, Larry, it's been a long time since we got to see you! So how's the world been treating you?"

"Subjectively speaking, I find my ephemeral pursuits in the world to be non-informative and too reticular for any evaluation, Uncle Tom."

"Oh."

Becoming increasingly addicted to my intellectual pursuits, I thought to myself, If a man isn't satisfied, it is primarily because he hasn't developed his mental potential. The more educated one becomes, the more one knows about life, well, then it only follows, the happier he'll be.

I was firmly convinced that education was the answer to man's search for happiness. I was also convinced that in order to further expand my intellect, I would have to increase my outside reading. So in addition to my college texts, I began to read numerous philosophy and psychology books. To broaden my perspective on contemporary literature, I tried to read one best-seller a week along the order of *The Autobiography of Malcolm X* and *Soul on Ice*. In keeping pace with current events, I subscribed to *Time*, *Newsweek*, *Life*, *Atlantic Monthly*, and numerous other publications, and read every article with keen interest.

"Larry, slow down!" Mom pleaded, as I gulped my breakfast. "You're going to kill yourself going at this pace!! How long do you—"

Bang! The door slammed behind me, and I was on my way again. The burnt orange Fiat 850 sports car that I had just purchased—in line with my *new* image—was perfect for weaving in and out of morning traffic on the way downtown to CSU.

My heart was beating doubletime, my sleep was spasmodic —usually about four hours a night—but I couldn't stop. Over and over I kept telling myself, "Diamonds are pieces of coal that stuck to their jobs. Diamonds are pieces . . ."

Life was moving at a hurricane pace, and at times I felt like I was about to fly apart, like an out-of-balance magneto. At those times, I would reassure myself. "Just hang on a little bit longer," I repeated over and over.

"I am going to make it this time—no matter what," I said aloud one day, wheeling into the center lane. "I'm going to be that Student Government President. This is it . . . it's got to be . . . where else am I going to look? . . . *Peace and purpose in life are going to be mine!*" And I slammed the steering wheel for emphasis. But even as I did so, I wondered . . .

Weight lifting, rock music, and booze had proven dead ends. And now the intellectual game was beginning to alienate acquaintances, and making me realize the futility of trying to keep pace.

A position of power seemed to be the only remaining answer.

Like all my peers, I was searching for identity and a way to eliminate that deep vacuum inside. While some of my friends were looking to drugs, the occult, and illicit sex for an answer, for some inexplicable reason, I was never drawn in those directions. Perhaps all that childhood training had left its mark on my conscience, after all.

Christmas Day, 1969, was less than a month away, yet never had the religious significance of the holiday meant so little. My ambitions and aspirations were firmly grounded in the world. I was a realist.

No great incident had destroyed my faith; it was something I had grown out of, like belief in Santa Claus—a comforting myth, nice to believe, but unfortunately not in line with reality and the facts of life.

I did not deny the existence of God, but to me, God was a great cosmic consciousness coming out of all nature. Determined to remain fair, I did divorce God from all the rules, rituals, and regulations that I had once been forced to abide by and which I thought had represented Him.

In my academic environment, my agnostic suspicions had been crystallized by intellectual arguments. Psychology, philosophy, and anthropology all seemed to agree that the concept of a personal God was a figment of unenlightened imaginations. Having seen no contrary evidence, I simply put the subject of God out of my thoughts.

CHAPTER

5

DECEMBER, the fifth—in a little over three weeks it would be the start of a new decade.

Driving to college on the heavily congested freeway in my new little convertible, I sat relaxed as my headlights pierced the morning darkness. A small leak in the convertible top was irritating me, as periodic raindrops kept falling on my new, pin-striped suit coat. "Rain continuing throughout the morning," the WKYC newsman said over the radio, "with partial clearing expected around noon. Have a nice day!"

That is exactly what I intended to do—until suddenly the red light under my speedometer flashed on, signaling car trouble. "What the . . ." I was extremely unknowledgeable about the workings of automobiles. Frantically flipping through the owner's manual as I drove, I surmised the problem was probably the generator.

"Damn it! This is a new car! These things aren't supposed to happen so soon!"

Slowly the speedometer needle inched its way leftward down the mileage scale until it hit bottom. No sooner had the car come to a stop in the middle lane of the freeway, than the surrounding auto horns began their barrage. Looking in the rearview mirror, I saw the animated silhouette of the motorist behind me; fists clenched and head bobbing, he obviously had a message for me.

"Ah, shut up, stupid! There's nothing I can do. Go around. *Go around!*" I yelled, as I waved my arm out the window.

Finally, I got out of the car into the cold, thirty-five degree rain and began pushing my car toward the gravel lane adjacent to the freeway. In seconds I was soaked through, and as I struggled along, I looked at the traffic jam I'd caused; in less than five minutes it had already backed up one mile.

The car's hood was steaming in the rain, and so was I. Obscenities flapped from my mouth like bats leaving a cave, and the hostile stares of passing motorists added coal to the fire.

"Beep-beep! . . . Honk! . . . Beep! . . ."

"Ah, shut up! *Shut up!*"

Three and a half hours later, an exasperated, infuriated, and thoroughly waterlogged young man stood dejectedly on the corner of Cleveland's East 55th and Saint Clair Avenue, his thumb extended. In the distance was my uplifted car, securely hooked to the rear of a towtruck.

Not having a raincoat or an umbrella, I had tucked my textbooks under my arm inside my drenched, disheveled suit coat.

Behind me was a vacant lot, the neighborhood dumping grounds. An old 1957 Chevy, stripped of all four tires, was parked in the center of the lot. Two young black children were crawling around inside the car, which provided them shelter from the rain.

"Going down, sir?" I questioned each motorist who stopped at the light. My plastic smile became more and more brittle with each successive "Sorry!"

"What the hell's the matter with people today?" I asked myself. "Can't they see I'm drowned?"

"Excuse me," I said politely as I became bolder and tapped lightly on a car window. "Are you going toward Cleveland State?"

The Lost Souls band, 1967 . . .

. . . and their drummer.

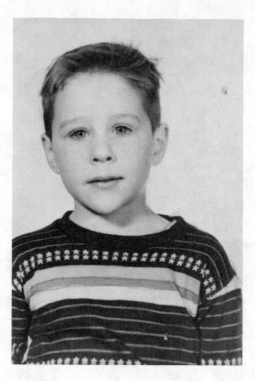

Parochial school days.

The transformed Tomczak family:
Dad, Mom, Sis, and Larry.

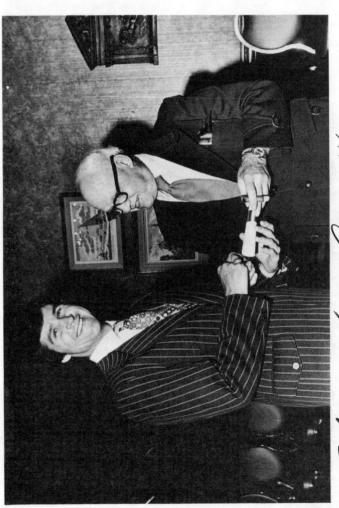

To Tony from George Meany

The author being congratulated by AFL-CIO President, George Meany.

Evangelist Larry Tomczak at Jesus '73 (a midsummer festival in the Pennsylvania countryside).

Pretending not to hear me, the obviously well-to-do middle-aged man twiddled his fingers on the steering wheel and anxiously awaited the green light. I asked louder.

"Excuse me! Could I have a lift, please?"

Feigning surprise as he turned his head, he scrutinized me for a second, frowned, and quickly motioned with his index finger that he would be turning at the next street. "Sorry," he said.

His shiny Continental pulled away, and I backtracked onto the curb and watched him pass eight successive streets before finally disappearing from sight, still headed downtown. The raindrops seemed to sizzle as they landed on the back of my neck.

After twenty minutes of failure, I was on the verge of beginning to walk the thirty blocks to CSU when an old, faded, gray, rusted and dented 1960 Comet slushed through the curbside puddles in my direction.

Maybe, just maybe . . .

"He's stopping! He's actually stopping!" I shouted in the rain. "Holy Toledo—a *miracle!"*

As the car came to a halt, the driver, a chunky, shorthaired, black gentleman of about fifty, extended a friendly wave from behind the partially steamed window and reached across the seat to open the door.

"How far you going?" he inquired.

"To Cleveland State—corner of 24th Street. You going that far?"

"Sure," he said as we pulled away. "If you can stand the exhaust fumes, I can sure use the company!"

Pulling my half-soaked books from under my coat, I saw puddles spreading on the floor mat under my feet.

I opened my mouth to offer a few feeble words of apology but quickly realized that it wasn't necessary. The man had already noticed my flood, but was grinning cheerfully.

The old Comet chugged along as we exchanged pleasantries; then a polite silence settled in until we came to within a few blocks of the University and stopped for a red light.

"Son—"

"Huh?" I said, turning. He was looking at me with such a softness in his face that it really got to me.

"Son, have you accepted Jesus Christ as your personal Savior?"

"*What?*"

"Have you accepted Jesus Christ as your personal Savior?"

Oh, man, I thought, what *is* this? But after what he'd done for me, I couldn't hurt his feelings. "Ah . . . yeah . . . I believe in God. I go to church."

"That's not what I asked you, son. Have you *personally* received Jesus Christ into your life as your Lord and Savior?"

He was looking at me with such solemnity that I had to say something. "Sir, I guess I don't understand what you're talking about; I'm really sorry."

He closed his eyes for a moment. The light changed and we went on in silence until we arrived at CSU.

"Well, thank you, really, very much for the lift," I said, opening the door.

"Son, I'd like to ask you to be my guest at our church service this Sunday morning. All the information is on this flier," he said, handing me a small pink paper. "Could you come?"

His bright smile, the twinkle in his eye, and the kindness he had shown me left no choice. "Okay, I'll try to make it."

"You *will?*" It was his turn to be startled.

"Mister, you picked me up when no one else would even stop. So if my car is fixed, I'll be there!"

He nodded, and we shook on it. Closing the car door, I slipped the flier into my hip pocket and darted for the CSU cafeteria. The rain had stopped, and the temperature felt slightly warmer as I caught a final glimpse of the old, beat-up

Comet pulling away, its driver looking up at the sky and grinning.

Six hours later I stood in our dining room where my sister was setting my mother's hair. Dad was reading the newspaper in the living room and, as usual, was not to be disturbed. The strong smell from the hair-setting solution caused me to cough a few times as I told Mom about my day.

"It was sickening being stuck out in that stupid rush-hour traffic," I said, "and, man, the people could have cared less."

"Well, just thank God that you weren't in any accident," Mom replied. "I shudder to think how your father would have reacted with his own lack of patience."

"The black fellow who picked me up," I continued, "was really nice. He took me down the rest of the way to CSU."

I was just about to go to my bedroom to change when it dawned on me that I had promised my black benefactor I would go to his church on Sunday. Pulling out the crumpled flier, I slipped it onto Mom's lap and said, "I don't think I'm going to be at Mass on Sunday. I told him I would go to *his* church."

Mom read the flier aloud slowly and deliberately.

GRACE PENTECOSTAL CHURCH OF JESUS CHRIST
EAST 55th AND HOUGH AVENUE
CLEVELAND, OHIO
SUNDAY WORSHIP—9:45 A.M.
"BRING A FRIEND"

Mom brushed my sister's hand away from her hair and raised her head. "Larry, you mean you're *not* going to Mass on Sunday?"

"Well, I've never missed before, but I am going to miss just once."

Tears collected in the corners of Mom's eyes as she slowly stood up, placed her hands on my shoulders, and said in almost a whisper, "But Larry, you can't! If you miss Mass, you will commit a *mortal sin. You will go to hell!*"

The statement hit hard. Finally, a few words came. "Well, I know, but—I promised this guy. I'll go to confession on Monday."

Just then Dad sprang from his chair and charged into the dining room. Grabbing the flier, he yelled loud enough to be heard for eight blocks: "Pentecostal Church! 55th and Hough! You're *not* going down to *that* ghetto neighborhood— That's where they had those riots! *Over my dead body you're going down there!*"

"Forget it!" I shouted and stalked off to my bedroom, throwing the door shut so hard that it shook the house.

Partly out of a sense of commitment and partly out of sheer rebellion, I drove down to 55th and Hough that Sunday morning. For all of twenty minutes, I rode up and down 55th Street looking for the church. My eyes searched the poverty-stricken milieu for a towering steeple, a big cross, granite stairs, the congested parking lot, an announcement board, anything that would identify a holy edifice. The more intently I looked, the more discouraged I became.

Finally I parked my car, locked it, and continued my search on foot. As I walked down the street, I realized why the Hough area was labeled a ghetto. Dilapidated apartment buildings and abandoned stores were everywhere. The aching eyes and forlorn expressions on the faces of the people I passed said it all. Hopscotching over a few garbage can lids lying on the sidewalk, I bent to tie my shoelace. As I did, my eyes caught a pack of a dozen rats or so crawling under a broken wood fence, and I shuddered.

Walking for two blocks, I finally came upon what appeared to be a little delicatessen in sore need of a paint job. The front window had a crack in it, and a strip of black tape was holding the pane intact. A small cross was carved on the old wooden door, and some hand-painted letters below proclaimed, *Grace Pentecostal Church of Jesus Christ.*

I'd better get out of here, I said to myself. This is no

church—this is a store! What the heck did that guy ask me to come *here* for?

Abruptly the door opened and out came an elderly black woman with a wailing baby in one hand and a Bible in the other. She left the door open, and I was able to peer inside.

The room, no larger than a single garage, had a wooden floor and was occupied by about twenty-five black people, a third of them little children. The people were sitting on four pairs of peeling, well-used benches neatly arranged before a timeworn pulpit situated at the front of the room. The only religious symbol I could find was a solitary cross that hung suspended on the wall behind the pulpit, a cross without any corpus.

I was just about ready to get out of there when some of the adults turned around and saw me standing in the doorway. Before I could even blink, two smiling women and a man came out, enthusiastically shook my hand, *hugged* me, and welcomed me. "God bless you, brother; it is so good to have you with us!"

I was speechless. Before I knew what was happening, I was being escorted down the narrow center aisle. That I was the only white person there did not seem to concern anyone.

These people made me feel like a visiting dignitary, as I was greeted by warm smiles, embraces, and handshakes. "Good morning, may the Lord bless you today!" so many of them said. Sitting down in the second row, I found myself between a tall, lanky, middle-aged gentleman with a crew cut and a short heavyset grandmother with graying hair and wire-rimmed glasses. Both of them embraced me and said, "God bless you, brother!"

"Ah . . . yes . . . ah, God bless you, too," I managed.

Handing me a hymnal, they began a song that I had never heard before:

> Amazing grace, how sweet the sound,
> that saved a wretch like me.

I once was lost but now I'm found,
was blind but now I see.

I couldn't believe how happy everyone seemed. Everyone was singing, joyfully, like they really meant it!

Then I got a shock. They started clapping along with the music. *Clapping their hands in church!*

The little grandmother at my side suddenly nudged me with her elbow.

"Come on, honey, clap those hands!" she said with a wink and a nod of her head.

"I . . . I couldn't."

Broadening her smile, she nudged me again, this time a little more firmly.

"Well . . . gee . . . I've always been taught that—"

"We are *commanded* to clap our hands," she said, with surprising authority.

"By whom?"

"By God!"

"Huh?"

"The Bible says, 'Clap your hands, all ye people, shout to God with loud songs of joy.' *That's God's word!*"

"Oh."

"Well," she said, nudging me in the ribs for a third time, "let's obey God!"

With great reluctance, I began clapping along with the song, feeling acutely ill-at-ease. Yet before the hymn was done, I found myself almost enjoying it. Say, this is kind of fun! I thought to myself. Whoever would have dreamed that church could be fun!

When we finished, the man on my left, whose skin was extremely dark, inquired, "Feel a little better?"

"Ah, yeah . . ."

"I don't believe I got your name; mine is Art."

"My name is Larry."

"You know, Larry," Art began, "God never intended His church to be a refrigerator to preserve piety. The Bible says we are to 'rejoice in the Lord *always.*' Look at Jesus—the Gospels show Him as a man of joy. He worked His first miracle at a wedding reception, and He said, 'I've come that you might have abundant life.' Jesus also said, 'I tell you these things that my joy might be in you and your joy might be perfect.' And don't forget His words: 'Be of good cheer.' "

"Ah . . . I guess I didn't know that, Art."

Art put his hand on my shoulder and laughed. His teeth were pearly white against his skin. "Larry, if you've accepted Jesus and feel His joy in your heart, you ought to notify your face!"

I obliged, feigned a chuckle, and brought forth a weak grin. If I've accepted Jesus . . . what the heck was he talking about?

As I pondered that, a young fellow behind me in his twenties, sporting a modified "Afro," spoke out: "Let us pray."

As I quickly looked around for a prayer book or card to follow, everyone in the little church began to pray spontaneously. They addressed Jesus Christ out loud and with such fervor that one would have thought that Jesus was actually there with them!

I bowed my head and eavesdropped on Art as he prayed. I had never heard such a prayer in my life—so simple and direct, so full of trust. Art really believed he was being heard, and listening to him, I began to wonder if maybe he was.

"Lord . . . Lord Jesus Christ, my Creator and my God. I thank You this morning for my salvation, for the gift of eternal life. I praise You for Your presence right here in this room . . ."

I jerked my head back at that and gave him a quick once-over.

"Jesus Christ," he continued, apparently unaware of my scrutiny, "in the Bible You say that whenever two or three gather together in Your name, You are there in the midst. Well, I honor You, Jesus, for that promise. Thank You, Lord. . . . I love you, Jesus. . . ."

As the people concluded their prayers, I heard someone coming up the aisle. I turned and saw the little black man who had picked me up when I was hitchhiking. He smiled at me as he walked up to the pulpit.

And did he preach! For forty minutes he drove it home: "Jesus Christ . . . Jesus Christ . . . Jesus Christ . . . Will you accept Jesus Christ into your life as your personal Savior? Make a commitment to Christ today, and accept the gift of eternal life."

He spoke so dynamically and sincerely that I never once took my eyes off of him. Talk about power! And authority! For a moment, he had me believing in heaven and hell again, like I hadn't since I was eight years old! In fact, I felt extremely uncomfortable, especially when he supported his statements with passages from the Bible.

At the end of his sermon, everyone lowered their heads, and as my preacher friend asked "that question" once more— "Will you accept Jesus . . ."—I sat in my place hushed and totally unaware of its significance for me.

In twenty minutes the service was completed, I had expressed my gratitude to the minister and the people, and was on my way home. I drove down 55th Street, deep in thought—about God.

I could not get rid of the minister's question—"Will you accept Jesus Christ into your life as your personal Savior?" I was haunted by these words; they seemed to be written on every passing car, on the pavement as I walked up the driveway, and across the sky as I paused and looked up before going inside.

For the remainder of the day, I was unable to think about anything else.

As much as I tried to placate my conscience on Monday,

there didn't seem to be anything I could do to dispel the prodigious guilt I felt for having missed Mass. *Mortal Sin— Hell—Mortal Sin—Damnation—Mortal Sin—Fire—* Throughout my morning classes, the words kept reappearing across my mind.

"This is crazy!" I said aloud, as I walked at noontime to the CSU Library. "I don't believe this bit about mortal sin, and yet, *damn it, I can't get it out of my mind!* Yet what if the Church is right, and I get killed before going to confession? I'd spend an eternity in hell just for missing one Mass. But then what about all the millions who aren't Catholics, who never go to Mass, what happens to them? Are they condemned?"

I stopped abruptly in the middle of an alley. *"Damn it!"* I cried out, *"What kind of a God are you?"* Then I spun my head around and exhaled a sign of relief. No one was in sight.

Giving a swift kick to a piled-high garbage can, I jogged out of the alley. Two blocks away was the University Catholic Center. There I could find a priest and a confessional.

Within a few days, my ego was again secure on the throne of the kingdom of self, and the recent disturbance at the gates was rapidly becoming a vague memory. My schedule was so frantic that all I had to do was resume it, and there was no more time for thinking about anything.

It was Wednesday when I found myself seated at a luncheon table in a luxurious restaurant in downtown Cleveland. Across from me was a man who represented more than one hundred fifty thousand union members and their families in the City of Cleveland—Mel Witt, the Community Services Director for the Cleveland AFL-CIO. Tanned and youthful looking for his fifty years, Mr. Witt had a pleasant voice with a slight Southern accent. His hospitality followed suit. He was most congenial and made me feel like a close friend, even insisting that I call him by his first name.

Our meeting concerned an assignment for the Cleveland

State Student Government. I had submitted a proposal to the
University that I felt could benefit the school, but more
important, gain for me the name-recognition I needed to win
the spring election. My idea was to unite college students and
"hard-hats" for community betterment projects. Mr. Witt had
been selected as my point of contact with the unions in the
City of Cleveland.

Waiting for our food to be served, I asked him about his
family.

"Well, Larry, I have one son about your age who's studying
for the ministry and another boy and girl who are in high
school. My wife has been working at our church as a secretary
to our minister. You ought to come out to our church
sometime."

"Yes, maybe someday I will."

I had no sooner finished what was intended to be merely a
courteous reply than Mr. Witt said, "How about this Sunday?"

"This *coming* Sunday?"

"Sure, why not?" he said with a radiant smile.

I knew that Mel Witt wasn't Catholic. The twenty-eight
hours of guilt I had experienced between missing Mass the
Sunday before and getting to confession was not something I
wanted to undergo again.

"I can't . . . I'd like to . . . but, you see, Mr. Witt—ah,
Mel—I have to attend my own service on Sunday morning."

He leaned back, took a sip of water, and said, "What are
you doing Sunday evening?"

"Nothing, I guess."

"Good! Come out to the house for dinner, and then we'll all
head out to church. We have a great service that starts at
seven, okay?"

I was trapped. Two church services in *one* day! I couldn't
believe it.

"Well?"

"All right," I said, trying not to sound glum. "Can you tell me how to get there? I'm not very familiar with the West Side."

As Mel drew a map on the back of a paper napkin, the waitress placed our food on the table. The aroma of the charcoal-broiled steak picked up my spirits.

What *is* this? I thought to myself. Two strange churches back to back— Something weird is happening, *really* weird.

This time I had sense enough not to share my plans with my parents, and late Sunday afternoon I slipped quietly out of the house. Following the directions on the paper napkin, I drove for forty minutes to the west side of Cleveland to Mel's house. After a sumptuous dinner, at which I envied how well they all got along together, we piled into Mel's car and headed for the church. The name of the church puzzled me—Bethel Temple. Was it a Jewish synagogue?

As we pulled into the driveway, the large brick church reminded me of a school gymnasium. A light blanket of snow covered the vast front lawn, in the center of which was a white announcement board topped by a massive brown cross. Again, there was no body on the cross.

We hung our coats on the racks in the lobby and moved through the two doors leading to the sanctuary. At the front of the auditorium on the elevated stage was a wooden pulpit with an organ to the left and a piano to the right. Directly behind the pulpit was a large wooden cross. No body on that one either, I noticed. And no statues anywhere.

We sat down in one of the back rows in the center section. Taking a quick glance at the hundreds of people in the congregation, I noted right away that a third to a half of the congregation consisted of high school and college-age youth. Tapping Mrs. Witt on the shoulder, I leaned sideways and whispered, "Did you come to church this morning?"

"Oh yes, and we had a *beautiful* service," she replied.

"What about these people? Were they in church this morning too?"

Mrs. Witt looked at me and said, "Yes, Larry, most everyone was here this morning. We love to come together and praise the Lord."

What kind of people are these? I wondered. Come to church twice in the same day, and they don't even have to? Must be fanatics! But they didn't look it.

Trying not to appear stupid, I again leaned toward Mrs. Witt and asked, "Did you say, 'Praise the Lord'?"

Mrs. Witt chuckled. "Oh, come now, Larry! You know what I mean! *Everyone* knows we are commanded to praise the Lord."

"We are? By whom?"

"God!"

"Huh?"

"The Bible teaches, 'Let everything that breathes praise the Lord.' As long as you're able to breathe, God wants you to praise Him."

Something was wrong—it had to be. "Mrs. Witt, what kind of church is this?"

"This is a Pentecostal church," she said, smiling.

Blam! Fireworks exploded in my head! The same kind of church as last week!

I turned to Mrs. Witt. "What exactly do you mean, Pentecostal?"

"Well, Larry, actually 'Pentecostal' is not a denomination. It refers to a spiritual way of life. People from all kinds of Christian churches—Baptists, Lutherans, Methodists, Episcopalians and many others—come together here to worship, especially on Sunday evening. A lot of Catholics come here, too! See that couple with the three kids up front in the second row? They're Catholics. So are many of the college kids. The important thing is not what label you wear, but whether or not you're a Christian."

Our conversation was interrupted as the congregation began jubilantly singing:

> I'm so happy here's the reason why,
> Jesus took my burdens all away!
> Now I'm singing as the days go by,
> Jesus took my burdens all away.

All of a sudden, the people started clapping in tempo with the peppy melody, and they started walking around and hugging each other and shaking hands and laughing—in church! Scores of people came up to me and embraced me and said, "God bless you, brother! Praise the Lord!"

I didn't know what to do . . . how to react . . . what to say. A brawny fellow in his late twenties threw his arms around me like I was a long-lost relative. Whatever else I may have thought, I knew that every overture was made in absolute sincerity. The people really cared about me. All over the church, people of all ages were smiling and singing and clapping and literally radiating joy. *Look at these people enjoying themselves in church! What is going on?*

"Sonny!" came a squeaky voice behind me.

Turning, I looked down to see a tiny white-haired eighty-year-old grandmother whose angelic-looking face was positively aglow. As she extended her arms, I realized she wanted me to bend forward. As I did, she rewarded me with a tender hug and a kiss on the cheek.

I couldn't think of anything to say, and I was annoyed that my eyes began to fill.

"We're glad you joined us tonight, son. You come back again, okay?"

I nodded and turned away.

Mrs. Witt anticipated my next query. "Yes, Larry, even that's in the Bible. God's Word tells us to greet the brethren with a holy kiss."

The ebullient singing continued for about twenty minutes but did little to soothe my unrest. The minister, Louis Davidson, then stepped to the pulpit. His thinning dark hair and deep-set eyes suggested a serious personality and a man of firm conviction. Tall and dressed in a conservative blue suit, he had a large Bible under his arm. As he bowed his head, he said, "Let's all remain standing for prayer."

People all over the church began to pray—out loud. Unable to resist, I looked up and saw many lifting their hands above their heads. This symbolic gesture of surrender to the Almighty heightened my uneasiness as I listened in on the prayers of those around me. Everyone was praying straight to Jesus, the same way they did in the ghetto church—as if He was actually present! And they were the same sort of prayers . . . sincere . . . real.

These people have something that I don't have, I thought. God is real to them. But why all the emphasis on *Jesus?*

The audible prayers of the congregation finally subsided; there were a few moments of silent meditation, and we took our seats. Unable to restrain my curiosity, I leaned toward Mrs. Witt again and asked, "Is lifting your hands in the Bible, too?"

"Sure! In both the Old and New Testaments. But don't worry about it. You pray however you feel most comfortable."

Just then, the minister asked if anyone had a testimony to share. Immediately a woman stood up and right in front of everyone told how after months of prayer, Jesus had healed her of terminal lung cancer. Next, a guy in his twenties, wearing jeans and shoulder-length hair, rolled up his sleeve to reveal dozens of needle marks on his arm. Tears came to his eyes as he told of three years of heroin addiction—

"Day after day after day, it was like living in hell! A hundred and fifty dollars a day for enough fixes to keep me from going out of my mind! And no one could help me—no one. I'd do *anything* for a fix—my body would explode if I didn't shoot up. And then one day, last month, a guy who had once been my source came by and told me how Jesus Christ had changed his life . . . had given him peace . . . had cured him of his own addiction and given him meaning in life. I laughed in his face and told him I didn't want any religion. He just kept telling me that he wasn't talking about religion, but about a person—Jesus Christ. In an hour, I was on my knees asking Jesus to come into my life. I cried out for a miracle, that He'd cure me of my addiction and save my soul. Well, I'm standing here to tell you that Jesus answered my prayer! *He entered my life, saved me, and cured me instantly—without any withdrawal!*"

The ecstatic young man broke into tears, and began praising God, and most of the congregation joined him. Without thinking what I was doing, I bowed my head and said, "Thank You, Jesus."

After the testimonies, Pastor Davidson invited the people to follow along in their Bibles as he read a passage from the "Word of God." And then he began to preach. His sermon was almost identical to that of the black pastor I had heard the week before. Like last week, there was no written-out sermon, not even notes.

The power was the same, and the authority. So was the question: "Will you accept Jesus Christ into your life as your personal Savior? Make your decision for Christ this night. Receive Him into your heart!"

That does it! I'm not leaving here till I find out what they're talking about.

Directly after the service, I went up to Pastor Davidson.

"Hello," he said, reaching out his hand.

"Mister Davidson, my name is Larry Tomczak, and this is my first time here. I came with the Witts. I really enjoyed this service tonight, but could I ask you something?"

"Sure."

"Well . . . I . . . ah . . . I don't really know what you mean by 'receiving Christ into your life.' You said it a lot tonight in your sermon."

His deep-set eyes met mine and he said, "Larry, do you read the Bible?"

"No, but I used to read a missal."

"Larry, have you *ever* read the Bible?"

"No."

"Do you *have* a Bible?"

"Well, yeah, we have a Bible in our home." And we did, too, but for over twenty years it had sat on a shelf. Mom and Dad had received it for a wedding present and used it for storing their marriage document, our birth certificates, and some other papers. But I could never tell him that.

Just then Mrs. Witt walked up and handed me a pocket-sized New Testament. "Thought you might be needing this," she said.

Pastor Davidson suggested some specific Bible passages for me to read, and I jotted down the chapters and verses inside the back cover.

"You know," he said, "I am not interested primarily in having people join our church. But I *am* interested in helping people discover Jesus Christ and the abundant and eternal life that comes from a personal relationship with Him. Jesus offers this life as a *gift* to every human being. This is what Christianity is all about. It's not a religion; it's a personal relationship with a risen, living Lord. But only *you* can make the decision to enter into the relationship by inviting Christ into your heart and accepting His free gift of eternal life. No church, no clergyman or parent can do it for you."

He paused and motioned us to a couple of seats on the side aisle. "Larry, let me ask you something— Are you a Christian?"

"Well, yeah . . . I mean, I guess so."

"What makes you a Christian?"

"Well, I . . . I belong to a church."

"So does a steeple, Larry."

"Huh?" I looked at him carefully, but he wasn't putting me down.

"Just because a person is born in a Christian church or a

'Christian' country, that doesn't make him a Christian, any more than being born in a garage makes him an automobile. The Bible says, 'To as many as *receive* Him, to them God gave the power to become children of God.'

"Christianity involves a personal decision to 'receive' Christ into your life. It's a decision you have to make for yourself. God has no grandchildren!"

The look of bewilderment on my face brought a gentle grin to his.

"Let me put it another way: a man isn't a soldier because he wears a uniform, or carries a gun, or carries a canteen. He is a soldier when he takes the enlistment oath. All the other things can be bought without enlisting. A church membership doesn't make one a Christian any more than owning a piano makes one a musician. Public, definite enlistment for Christ is what makes you a Christian. You can join a church, give faithfully in the collection, attend the services, return thanks, and do everything that would apparently stamp you as a Christian— even pray—but you won't ever *be* a Christian, until you do what God tells you to do."

"But, Mister Davidson," I said, getting up, "I don't know what God wants me to do!"

"Don't get uptight, Larry. The Bible says, 'Believe on the Lord Jesus Christ in your heart and confess Him with your mouth and you will be saved.' That's in Saint Paul's letter to the believers in Rome. God has the same plan of salvation for everyone. It's His law—you may not approve of it, but that doesn't make any difference."

I laughed and sat down again.

"If you were sick, Larry, all the medicine *I* might take wouldn't do *you* any good. Salvation is a personal matter that no one else can do for you; you must attend to it yourself. *You've* got to decide whether you will receive Christ into your life."

I was silent for a moment. Then I said, "I don't *have* to confess with my mouth, do I?"

"Larry, m-o-u-t-h doesn't spell *intellect*. If I was outside your door, and you wanted me to enter, you'd use your voice to invite me in. It's the same way with Christ. Jesus says, 'Behold, I stand at the door, and knock: if any man hear my voice, and open the door, I will come in to him.' Jesus will never barge into your life. But He will come in if you ask Him."

"But isn't that a little childish?" I argued, a little desperately.

Pastor Davidson wasn't smiling. Putting a hand on my shoulder, he said, "Son, Jesus told us unless we become like little children, we will not enter the Kingdom of God. We can't come to Christ by intellect alone. You *have* to come by faith, as a simple, little child would come." He paused. "And when you do, He comes into your heart, He forgives your sins, He adopts you into His family, and you become a child of God.

"That's the road, and it's the only one mapped out for you and me. God treats us all alike. He doesn't furnish one plan for a banker and another for the janitor who sweeps out the bank. The way to salvation is not Harvard, Yale, or even Cleveland State."

My head seemed to be spinning, but the picture was beginning to come clear.

"If what you're saying is true," I said, "then all these years I've been bitter and running from God—from Jesus Christ—because of some bad religious experiences I've had."

He laughed as I shook my head in perplexity. "Don't worry about it, Larry. You're one of millions who know religion but haven't yet experienced God in the only way we can experience Him—in the person of His Son, Jesus Christ."

"Jesus is kind of like God spelling Himself out in language that man can understand, huh?" I said.

"Yes, I suppose that's one way of putting it," Pastor

Davidson said. "One last thing: the quickest way to get to know Jesus is to read the accounts and letters of His original disciples. Larry, if you go home and start reading from the Word of God, I can assure you that everything will begin to make sense."

I tucked my New Testament in my hip pocket and left Bethel Temple with the Witts, eager to get home and start my reading.

In less than an hour, I was sitting at my old wooden desk reading about a Person who wanted to give me eternal life. For years the Gospels had gone in one ear and out the other as they were read during Mass. Yet now, as I read each living word, the person of Jesus was coming alive.

Finally, at the end of the Gospel of John, I looked up at the clock on the wall: 2:45 A.M.

Leaning back in my chair, I closed my eyes and tried to hold back tears that were welling up. Turning out the light, I sat in a sea of darkened tranquillity. And in a whisper, I began to pray.

"God, it's been so long since I've really talked to You. I'm sorry. Yet somehow it's all different tonight.

"All my life I've felt that You were high and holy and unreachable; that's why I gave up on You. And now I see that all my life You've been waiting for me to realize how much You loved me. Oh, Jesus, I want Your love . . . I will come unto You. Please, help me, Jesus . . . please."

And I wept—like I hadn't since I was a little child.

I don't know how long I sat there in the darkness. Gradually, the tears subsided, and a sense of deep peace settled over me, a peace so complete, so perfect and unbroken, I hardly dared breathe. In my heart, I knew that everything was different now, for He had heard. And I knew something else for a certainty: He was there in the dark with me.

I whispered His name—and grinned, knowing that He

heard. I did it again. He seemed to want me to give Him the hurts in my life, and like a kid reaching into the toy box to show a loving father one broken toy after another, for Him to make them whole, I put them in His hands.

Then I wanted to tell Him about the very worst sins I had committed and ask Him to forgive me. I did, and He did. And I felt clean, all the way through my being—for the first time in my life.

"Jesus, Jesus, Jesus . . ." I shook my head, and the tears came again—tears of joy. I was beginning to know the wonder of His love.

Some time later, I turned the light back on. I had a voracious desire to get to know God better, much better. And fast.

I flipped ahead in the New Testament, and it fell open to Colossians. I read:

> Who is the image of the invisible God, the firstborn of every creature: For by him were all things created, that are in heaven, and that are in earth, visible and invisible, whether they be thrones, or dominions, or principalities, or powers: all things were created by him, and for him: And he is before all things, and by him all things consist. And he is the head of the body, the church: who is the beginning, the firstborn from the dead; that in all things he might have the preeminence. For it pleased the Father that in him should all fulness dwell.
>
> Colossians 1:15–19

So Jesus was God! The babe in the manger and the Creator of the universe were one and the same. And all my life I had been watering Him down!

Then I remembered the verses that Mr. Davidson had suggested I read. Looking each one up, I read them meticulously.

"Wait a minute; something isn't right here," I said under my breath. "I know what it is; this isn't a Catholic Bible!"

I tiptoed into our living room, reached up and took down our Catholic Bible, which looked brand-new in spite of the fact it was older than I was. Laying the Bibles side by side on my desk, I matched the Scripture with Scripture. I was dumbfounded. "They're the same!" I shouted.

"Larry," came the voice from my mom's bedroom, "go to sleep! It's three-thirty!"

"Sorry," I whispered. But I still couldn't believe it. For twenty years I'd believed that mechanical obedience to rules and laws would one day bring me eternal life. Now I read that eternal life is God's *free gift*—it depends on His *grace*, not my good works! There it was, before my eyes:

> The wages of sin is death, but the gift of God is eternal life through Jesus Christ our Lord.
>
> Romans 6:23

> For by grace are ye saved through faith; and that not of yourselves: it is the gift of God: Not of works, lest any man should boast.
>
> Ephesians 2:8–9

We were sinners, separated from God and His gift of eternal life.

> For all have sinned, and come short of the glory of God.
>
> Romans 3:23

Jesus Christ, the Son of God, was the *only* answer to this problem of separation. When Christ was crucified on the cross, He died in our place, as our substitute, paying the full penalty for all sin, thereby bridging the separation between God and man. We were saved by a person, by only *one* person.

> Jesus saith unto him, I am the way, the truth, and the life; no man cometh unto the Father, but by me.
>
> John 14:6

> For there is one God, and one mediator between God and men, the man Christ Jesus.

I Timothy 2:5

God had provided the only way. Man had to make the choice, to individually accept Jesus Christ as Lord and Savior.

But as many as received him, to them gave he power to become the sons of God, even to them that believe on his name.

John 1:12

Receive Him. So that's what they'd been talking about! He wants to enter my life and be my Savior; all He asks is that I yield myself to Him and receive Him by a personal invitation.

Behold, I stand at the door and knock: if any man hear my voice, and open the door, I will come in to him, and will sup with him, and he with me.

Revelation 3:20

But ye are not in the flesh, but in the Spirit, if so be that the Spirit of God dwell in you. Now if any man have not the Spirit of Christ, he is none of his.

Romans 8:9

He that hath the Son hath life; and he that hath not the Son of God hath not life.

I John 5:12

I sat motionless in the center of my room. All those years . . .

"Larry, it's four o'clock in the morning! What's going *on* in there?"

"Nothing, Mom . . . I was just having a bad dream." But the nightmare was over, and as I finally turned out the light, I sensed His presence again.

The next Sunday evening I returned to Bethel Temple. At the conclusion of the service, when Pastor Davidson invited anyone who wanted to receive Jesus into his life to come forward, I hesitated. "Does this mean I'll be rejecting my Catholicism?

"No, it can't. I'm not rejecting anything or anyone. I'm not joining another church, either."

I quietly joined the others at the front of the church. Kneeling down, I began to pray. I admitted that I was a sinner and could do nothing to save myself. I repented again of my sins and acknowledged that because Jesus was the Son of God, His death was full payment for those sins. And then I came to the part He was waiting to hear.

"Jesus, I want to receive You tonight as my Lord and Savior. I want You to come into my life right now. I surrender to You."

I remained on my knees, the tears trickling down my face. I was in Him now, and He in me, and I knew it. I became aware then of a passage of Scripture running through my mind, and knew it applied to me:

> Therefore if any man be in Christ, he is a new creature: old things are passed away; behold, all things are become new.
>
> II Corinthians 5:17

Gradually I became aware of a woman's voice rising to prominence above the rest of the assembly. Abruptly, the congregation seemed to be listening. I turned around where I was kneeling and concentrated on what she was saying. Her language was foreign to me, unlike any I had ever heard. Just as I spotted her in the second row along the hall, she uttered her final words. Her eyes were closed, and she obviously was absorbed in prayer. An interval of silence followed, and then an elderly gentleman seated a few feet away from me delivered a brief message in English, as if he had some direct inspiration about the meaning of what the woman said. When he finished, the congregation resumed their worship.

When the last song was over, I was standing before Pastor Davidson, awaiting his explanation for what I had just witnessed.

"Larry, in all four Gospels, John the Baptist said of Jesus,

'He will baptize you with the Holy Spirit.' Immediately before His ascension, our Lord said, 'Before many days you shall be baptized with the Holy Spirit.' He also said, 'You shall receive power when the Holy Spirit comes upon you; and you shall be my witnesses.' You remember what happened on Pentecost?"

"The Holy Spirit came down upon the believers in fulfillment of Christ's promise, right?"

"Yes, and what else?"

"All of those assembled began to speak in other tongues, didn't they?"

With a radiant smile, he nodded. "Larry, tonight when you surrendered your life to Christ, you opened yourself to a new life lived in the power of God through the Holy Spirit. Now, as you come to a *full* and *complete* surrender of yourself to Jesus Christ, He will allow the Holy Spirit to overflow in and through you by the action of faith in His promise to 'baptize you in the Holy Spirit.' As you yield more and more of yourself to the Spirit of God, your heart will be set aflame with love for Jesus, and you will more and more show forth His praise and power in your life."

My intellect did not grasp all that he was saying, or how it would come to pass, but already I had learned to listen with my heart and not my head.

"Being baptized in the Spirit means being introduced to an intimate, experiential relationship with the Holy Spirit, who will manifest His gifts in your life for the building up of the Body of Christ. Two of these gifts you witnessed here tonight—the gift of tongues and interpretation of tongues. The other spiritual gifts—prophecy, healing, working of miracles, faith, wisdom, knowledge, and discerning of spirits—are also tools which God has given for building the Church. But the New Testament will give you all the details. Keep reading!"

"Don't worry about that," I laughed. "It will be hard to stop long enough to study and work."

"Larry, there's one thing you should keep in mind: the

Baptism in the Holy Spirit is not an end in itself. Its main purpose is to enable and empower you to live the life that He has called you to live—which is impossible in the natural. We need *supernatural* power to live this new life, and we derive that power from the Holy Spirit. So remember to seek the Giver, not the gifts, okay?"

"I know one thing," I said, shaking his hand. "I'm going to *need* all the power I can get when I tell my family and friends what's happening to me!"

I could not have dreamed how true those words would prove to be.

6

"GET the hell out of my room, you fanatic!" My sister's hand was planted firmly in the small of my back, and she was propelling me toward the door for all she was worth.

"But Margaret," I pleaded, "I love you. Can't you at least give me a minute to explain what 'accepting Christ' means?"

"I told you—I don't want to hear any more of that crap!" *Slam!*

I had prayed for the entire week that the Lord would guide me in how and when to share my experience with my sister. And so, the first Sunday of 1970, one week following my surrender to Jesus, I climbed the stairs to Margaret's bedroom and knocked on the door.

To label Margaret's room "bizarre" would have been an understatement. In the center was an overhead lampshade from which hung yard-long strands of yellow beads. It was spray-painted a luminous green, and it cast a dim, eerie shadow over the entire room. The walls were painted in the same sour apple hue, and even though it was three-thirty in the afternoon, Margaret still had the shades fully drawn.

Eight medium-sized stuffed animals—a turtle, a duck, a few birds, and some monkeys—hung suspended from the ceiling, conveying the impression of a surrealistic zoo. In the far corner was a three-foot-tall, emerald green statue of the "Sitting

Buddha." A wisp of perfumed smoke slowly ascended from the incense tablet burning on Buddha's lap.

In the other corner of the room was a massive, six-foot-tall stuffed "Teddy" bear. One of its arms was resting atop an old cedar chest that Margaret used for storing all of her "souvenirs." Whenever Margaret went to a restaurant or hotel, she always felt entitled to a little memento of her visit. Whether it was silverware, dishes, glasses, or even a blanket, these items were all classified under Margaret's special category of "souvenirs."

Margaret, still in her nightgown, was lying on the bed, staring at the ceiling as I tried to talk to her. Her attitude was clearly conveyed by her growling, "Well, what do *you* want?"

"Margaret, something wonderful has happened to me!"

"Well, hooray for you!"

"Aw come on, Marg. Just listen, okay? It all centers around a person, Jesus Christ. He's real, and last week I accepted—"

"Look!" Margaret yelled. *"I go to Mass;* that's more than most of my friends do. And since when are you all of a sudden Goody-Two-Shoes?"

That did it; I blew it, but good, hurling accusations at her. "Yeah, you go to Mass, and then you go out and steal and get drunk. Why do you even bother going to church? Do you go because you love God or because you're afraid of committing a Mortal Sin?"

"All right, buster—out! *Get the hell out of here!"*

I went to my own room, and kneeling next to my bed, I began to weep.

"Lord, I blew it. I'm really sorry. But I'm scared for Margaret . . ."

I quieted down then and slowly realized that He loved Margaret and wanted her to come to Him even more than I did. And He seemed to assure me, then, that He was in control of the situation, and that I should be patient.

"Lord Jesus, forgive my impatience. I claim Margaret for Your Kingdom, and Mom and Dad, too, in the fullness of Your time. Please look after them, particularly Margaret when she's been drinking. In Your precious name I ask these things. Amen."

About a week and a half later, I drove home from CSU and found my father sitting down, looking out the dining-room window. Mom was shopping with Margaret, and I wondered if this might be the Lord's time for me to share Him with my father. He had apparently just gotten home from the bank where he was custodian and had been too tired to take off his blue uniform.

"What have you got there?" he asked, as I walked into the dining room.

"Huh?"

"The books under your arm—what are you reading these days?"

That was surely the signal! "Well, this first one is called *Pentecostalism*, but rather than get into that, let me show you this other book."

It was a thick paperback Catholic Bible—*The New American Bible*—that I had just purchased the previous day.

"The Bible?" Fanning the pages, he quickly handed it back like it was a hot potato. "What do you want with this?"

"Well, all I can say is, I've been studying it for the past month. And it's opened up a whole new world to me."

"Eh, the Bible's full of contradictions," Dad replied.

"Well, I haven't found any so far," I said, as I held out the Bible to him. "But here, show me one."

Dad turned away from my outstretched hand. "We're not supposed to read the Bible!"

I hit my thigh. Almost every Catholic I had spoken to about the Bible had said the same thing. The first few times I was at a loss for words, but within the past week I had done some research. Pulling a piece of paper from my Bible, I said, "Listen to this, Dad; this is a statement from the Second Vatican Council that was held in Rome, and Pope John signed it:

" 'This sacred Synod *earnestly* and *specifically* urges all the Christian faithful, especially religious, to learn by frequent reading of the Bible.' "

Dad said nothing, and I pressed on.

"The Roman Catholic Church is changing. It realizes that the Bible cannot be ignored any longer. Not only that, but it also is becoming aware that millions of Catholics have no real commitment to a living, risen Jesus Christ. They've never received Him into their hearts as a personal Savior."

"Received Him? A personal Savior? What are you talking about?" Dad asked. In my zeal, I was getting ahead of myself as well as Dad.

"I'm talking about the fact that just because you're born into a church, that doesn't make you a Christian."

"*What?*" Dad said. "I'm a *Catholic*, Larry!"

"So was Hitler, and Stalin was, too; he even studied for the priesthood."

"But I've been baptized," Father retorted.

"So were they! Here, let me read something else." I again referred to the piece of paper in my Bible. "Vatican II stated this:

" 'Baptism, of itself, is only a beginning, a point of departure. It is orientated toward a complete profession of faith . . . '

"See, Dad? Many Catholics are Catholic simply because they've never decided not to be. They go through the motions at Mass each week and get nothing out of it, because *God isn't real to them.* Going to Mass, praying, even reading the Bible are all boring if you don't know God personally, and there is only one way you *can* know Him personally—and that's through His Son, Jesus Christ."

"Since when did you get so religious?" Dad snapped.

"I haven't gotten religious," I pleaded. "I just found Jesus. I received Him as my Savior almost a month ago, and He's transforming my entire life. He's saved me and given me the gift of eternal life."

There! It was said! But my father didn't understand one word of it. Worse, I could tell by his lips twitching that he was about to blow his stack.

To calm us both down, I went to the refrigerator for a couple of bowls of chocolate-chip ice cream, his favorite snack. But it was too late. His words followed me into the kitchen.

"Look, young man, I'm almost sixty years old. *No twenty-year-old punk is going to tell me about my religion, understand?*"

"But Dad, look in your own Bible. Just check out . . . Dad . . . Dad . . . *Dad!*"

And the Tomczak front door terminated another memorable family discussion.

As my junior year at CSU drew to a close, I found myself alienated from many people whom I loved dearly. Margaret and Dad avoided me like a plague, both of them constantly referring to me as a fanatic and holy-roller. I slipped a few more times, but basically I was learning the painful lessons of silent patience.

I wasn't learning them as fast as Dad would have liked, however, and he was finally provoked to the point of telling me to "get the hell out of the house and go live with those religious fanatics." It was only through much prayer and the tearful intercession of my mother that he changed his mind.

It was always painful for me to see Mom cry, especially when it was on my behalf. It brought back memories of the years of suffering that she endured scrubbing floors on hands and knees so I could "have it as good as the rest of the kids."

"Why do you have to be so different from everybody else?" Mom kept asking. "Why can't you just be a good Catholic boy?"

Late one evening in March, I found myself standing in Mom's bedroom embroiled again in a futile discussion with Mom concerning Jesus. With tears streaming down her face, Mom sat in her cotton nightgown on the edge of her bed, entreating me, "Larry, please, please don't do this to us! Your father and I have worked so hard to bring you up in the *right* way. How can you reject your fine Catholic training, after we sent you through twelve years of Catholic school? How, Larry? How can you?"

"Aw Mom, don't cry. I haven't rejected anything; I've only made my commitment to Jesus. I'm still a Catholic! I go to Mass. I receive Communion. And they mean something to me now."

Mom blew her nose in the tissue that I handed to her. She looked at me through her puffed eyes and shook her head.

"Larry, see this rosary? I try to keep it with me always. Mary will take care of me. And she'll take care of you, too. She watches over our entire family. She always has. That's why her statue is on the front lawn.

"Whenever someone wants something on earth from his father, he'll always ask his mother, and she'll get it for him. That's how it is with Mary. She goes to God for us."

"But, Mom, I never come to you when I want something from Dad. I go straight to him. Over and over Jesus said, 'Come unto *Me*.' I love Mary, Mom, I always have. She's a model of humility and purity and obedience; but Jesus Christ is the God who created us—and He created Mary, too. He is our Savior—our one and only Savior. Even Mary acknowledged Him as her Savior. Remember her words at the Annunciation? 'My soul doth magnify the Lord, And my spirit hath rejoiced in God my *Saviour*' " (Luke 1:46–47).

Mom grabbed her rosary beads and clutched them tightly. I sat down next to her and put my arm around her. As I kissed her on her cheek, I tasted the salt from her tears.

"Mom, I don't want to upset you. I love you. You're the best Mom a guy could ever have. I just want to share with you the joy and peace I've found in a personal relationship with Jesus Christ. God is *alive* to me now . . . Mass is meaningful . . . prayer is exciting . . . Jesus Christ has taken up residence in my heart!"

Mother closed her eyes, as if her not looking at me would make me hush. Not wanting to give up, I continued, "Mom, you know in the Mass when we say 'Lamb of God who takes away the sin of the world,' what we're saying is that Jesus was sacrificed as a lamb to be the one and only sacrifice for the world's sin. That's what Holy Communion at Mass is all about. Every time we eat the host, we are remembering the body of Christ nailed to the cross for us, and every time we drink the wine, we are remembering the blood that was shed on the cross as a covering for our sins.

"Christ's atonement for our sins is sufficient because God said it was. My sin was committed against God. If God is content with what Christ has done on my behalf and is willing to pardon me, then I have nothing more to worry about. I am redeemed! I am reconciled! I am assured of heaven—but not because of any good works of my own. I deserve to go to hell, but *Jesus Christ went to hell for me on that cross!* God permitted His Son to sacrifice Himself on my behalf and God accepted His sacrifice when He died. Now all God asks us to do is receive His Son into our heart—to trust Him for our salvation—and He assures us of eternal life. It's a free gift! Isn't that good news? That's what 'Gospel' means—good news!"

Mother shook my arm off her shoulder. "It's eleven-thirty, Larry—I've got to get to bed."

Turning off the light, Mom pulled the covers partially over her head and rolled over on her side.

In tears, I walked out of her room and went to my own.

During the next half a year, very little changed in our home. Daily I studied my Bible and prayed for my family, relatives, friends, and my Church. Although they couldn't help being aware of the change in my life, Dad, Mom, and Margaret still avoided any discussion centered around Christ.

At Cleveland State University, the election for Student Body President was held a few weeks prior to summer recess. Having prayed for and received confirmation that I was to run for the position, I did, and was elected by 78 percent of the vote. With almost fourteen thousand students to represent, I sensed God had a plan to unfold in the coming academic year.

Nearly half of CSU was Catholic, and approximately 75 percent of those fallen away—exactly as I had been less than a year ago. Wherever I went, I tried to witness for Jesus Christ. I had little trouble initiating conversations for the Lord. But most of the time my witnessing fell on deaf ears.

Invariably the reaction from young Catholics was the same: "Look, I told you, I had *enough religion* in grade school!" From the adults it was always, "Look, I told you, I go to Mass!"

One particularly hot and humid Sunday in August, I was at Mass, and having taken Communion, I was letting my mind wander back to my own parochial years— The Church had most of us only until the eighth grade. We accepted what we were told on faith and proved our love of God by obedience to Church rules.

Eventually, as we grew older and were taught to question things, we began to question some of the rules. If I miss Mass, will I really go to hell? Is there really such a place as Purgatory, and can I really earn time off then for good behavior now?

After being questioned, many of the rules were inevitably rejected. But since our relationship with God was based solely on our relationship with Church and our ability to obey its rules, then rejection of Church rules meant rejection of God.

Everybody was so uptight about all the kids who had turned off the Church, the steady increase of defections from the clergy, the millions who had given up their faith. The fact was we hadn't given up the faith at all; *we had never understood it!* What we gave up was our allegiance to what we had understood as only a noble, venerable, superstructure called the Roman Catholic Church. The question I felt like standing up and shouting was: What happened to Jesus Christ in this superstructure? What happened to the Church's original commission: to proclaim the Good News to everyone that they may have eternal life and that Jesus Christ, the Son of God, is the only answer to man's deepest needs?

Unless the Church quickly recovered its God-given mission, the present specter of millions of frustrated Catholics abandoning a once-august, fortress Church would accelerate, until what we were experiencing would seem mild compared with the earthquake to come.

Opening my eyes, I saw that the last communicants were going to the rail. Slowly I turned and looked at the faces of the people in Holy Cross Church. There were so many blank, lifeless, despairing expressions.

We were a people starving for a heartwarming, personal faith, a vital experience with Jesus Christ. Yet who would listen to me—a twenty-year-old kid? If only the Pope could be reached. . . .

I could see myself standing before the Pope in a spacious, ornate red-carpeted room in the Vatican. On his elevated papal dais, the Holy Father would be seated in the massive, antique Chair of Saint Peter over which hangs the yellow and white Papal Flag with its two crossed keys representing the power and supremacy handed down from the Apostle Peter.

Magnificently garbed in red and white flowing vestments, head adorned with the triple crown indicating his sovereignty, his golden shepherd's staff in his left hand, the Pope would slowly lift his right hand to bestow on me his blessing. Before bowing, I would catch a glimpse of the resplendent Ring of Saint Peter on his finger.

In rising to my feet, I'd try not to be overwhelmed by all the majesty and ceremony. I'd clutch my Bible and look into his eyes and say, "Holy Father, we're in trouble, but we're not without hope. We still serve a living God who desires to rescue and restore the sinking ship."

He would nod, and I would continue, "Your Holiness, there are two things that I believe God is trying to tell His Church today, if we would only listen.

"First, our Church has got to begin calling its members into a personal relationship with Jesus Christ.

"Secondly, the Church has to explain and emphasize that it is by this relationship, and only by this relationship, that we receive God's free gift to mankind—eternal life. The observance of rules of the Church is our way of showing our love for God, not earning salvation.

"And we must start *now*. We cannot afford to ignore our millions of lost and strayed sheep a moment longer.

"I have eleven buddies, all Catholics, and eight are into drugs. Some of them into the real heavy stuff. If any one of them were here now, he would probably say what I would have said myself until I met Jesus eight months ago. They're sick of church, and to them, God is a million miles away, maybe even dead.

"I think I can imagine the enormous demands on your Holiness, and the rest of the Church hierarchy, but if you could only see—really *see*—what's happening to my generation. Every kid I know is searching for a way to fill the horrible void inside himself. Drugs, booze, promiscuity, activist rebellion, mobilized escape . . . anything to avoid confronting the emptiness inside them, the emptiness only a personal relationship to a living God can satisfy.

"And the occult explosion—young people, convinced of the existence of a supernatural reality, yet denied access to God by churches that have stopped spreading the Good News, are turning to Satan as never before in history. Same thing with the Eastern religions—sure, they're just elaborate head-traps, but they're succeeding because they seem to offer *something*.

"And more and more young people cannot find *anything* in the world to fill the void and simply decide to put an end to it all. I don't know how serious suicide is here in Italy, Holy Father, but in the United States, it is the second leading cause of death among adolescents.

"We're searching. Yet what do we get? More innovations—a folk Mass, an alternative Saturday evening Mass, a community Mass, a young people's Mass, the sign of peace, parish councils, and married deacons. A cry for more relevancy—inner-city priests, plainly dressed bishops and nuns, religious involvement in peace demonstrations, sermons on social issues, clergymen in politics, and a whole busload of other things.

"Some feel parishioners have to be entertained with multimedia presentations—slides and records—during sermons, or guitar solos during Communion.

"But the innovations, the involvement, the entertainment are not working. People aren't coming back to the Church. The exodus is not slowing down.

"Because there is only one answer: personal relationship with Jesus Christ. Give them that, and not only will you have all your flock back, you will have to triple the number of Masses and raise up new cathedrals to accommodate all the *new* people."

I felt a tap on my shoulder and realized that while I was talking to the Pope in Rome, everyone else at Holy Cross had stood for the last blessing.

"The Mass has ended, go in peace to love and serve the Lord."

Things were going better with my family by the end of that summer. Slowly, painfully, I had learned a few things about patience, and that many times the most loving thing was to say nothing at all. Even my father grudgingly acknowledged the change. "Have to admit something's different," he'd say to Mom.

It still wasn't easy to control my once-volatile temper, but God gave me the supernatural strength that I needed. On one occasion I almost blew it when I had to ask my sister for a favor. I needed a lift, and standing in the kitchen munching on a leg of chicken, Margaret shook the drumstick in my face as she warned, "I'll take you! But just listen to me, buster! You say the name of Jesus just once along the way, I'll stop the car and throw you out on your ear, understand?"

I understood. So did Jesus, who granted me the grace not to respond in kind.

At midnight on September 6, 1970, the Sunday before my twenty-first birthday, I suddenly sat up in bed, with the strong sense that the Lord had awakened me. I got up, was led to tiptoe into my parents' bedroom, and stood there between their beds, barely able to make them out from the light in the hall. Dad was curled up like a bear with his face to the wall, while Mother lay on her back, the covers pulled up to the tip of her nose.

The only sound was their soft, slow breathing.

Looking down at them, I felt a steadily deepening sense of conviction as to how much my parents had sacrificed—so I could be raised in a decent neighborhood and go to good schools "like the other kids."

As I looked at Dad, I remembered when I used to crawl up on his bed on Sunday mornings and hug him while he slept. He was sixty years old now, drawing to that day when he'd put on his blue uniform for the last time.

He had never owned a car, choosing to invest the money in the education of my sister and me. Every day for over a decade, in all kinds of weather, Dad walked over five miles to and from his work. He used to go to a local barber college in order to save a buck on his haircuts.

"I love you, Dad," I whispered, choking up. "Thank You, Jesus, for him."

Turning my head, I looked over at my mother. Some of her wrinkles had come during the seven years she scrubbed floors on her hands and knees while suffering her painful hip affliction.

"She did that for me, Lord," I said softly.

I closed my eyes and prayed, "Jesus, You had a Mother. You loved her and provided for her. Jesus, provide for my Mother, too. Break down any barriers in the way of my Mother coming into a full relationship with You. Empower me with Your Holy Spirit so I can witness the Good News 'in Spirit and in Truth.' In Your name I pray. Amen."

I slipped out of their room and went back to bed. Before I dozed off, one passage of Scripture came repeatedly to my mind: "Ye shall receive power, after that the Holy Ghost is come upon you: and ye shall be witnesses unto me, both in Jerusalem, and in all Judaea, and in Samaria, and unto the uttermost part of the earth" (Acts 1:8).

Almost nine months had passed since my decision for Christ and my initial exposure to the Baptism in the Holy Spirit. Although I prayed almost nightly for Jesus to bestow on me this wonderful Baptism, nothing happened.

A week later, on my twenty-first birthday, at 11:00 P.M., I was on my way home from the Sunday evening service at Bethel Temple. Having met a number of young Catholic believers that night, I was full of joy despite the driving rain.

For the first time in over a month, I had gone alone. Dennis Marek, my turned-off Catholic friend who had played lead guitar in our rock band, had been coming to the evening services with me. Enchanted by the loving atmosphere and spontaneity of worship, and being confronted by the reality of who Jesus was, Dennis accepted Christ into his life the second time he came. He was enthralled by the Bible and wrote two songs about Jesus and shared them with the delighted congregation.

But this particular night, Dennis had not been feeling well and had stayed at home. As I drove down his street, it occurred to me that he might still be up, so I stopped by.

He had been making some recordings on his tape recorder and seemed glad to see me.

He extended his hand and said, "Well, happy birthday! So now you're a man, huh?"

For half an hour, we visited in the garage. He toyed with the recorder, while I sat on a lawn chair, feet atop his bicycle, and talked about the evening's service.

"Hey, what gives in there?"

Walking up the driveway out of the rain was Denny Carleton. I had not seen Denny much since our Lost Souls had collapsed. The last I had heard of him, he had dropped out of college and was spaced-out in another rock group.

As Denny entered the garage, his shoulder-length, blond hair was soaked from the rain, and he pushed it behind his ears. Wearing a pair of striped flares, tennis shoes, and a gold turtle-neck sweater, he did not look much different from the last time I saw him.

"Denny, it's been about a year, hasn't it?" I said, shaking hands.

"Yeah, guess so. Man, I don't even remember when we last talked."

"So what brought you over here in this kind of weather?" Dennis Marek asked.

"Well, I was going by and noticed you guys in the garage, so I stopped to find out what's been happening. What have you been doing with your life, Larry?"

As I sat back down in the lawn chair, I felt my heart skip a beat. I'd have to tell him about Jesus. Of all people to have to witness to . . . he'll probably laugh right in my face . . . why did he have to come here tonight?

"Denny, ah, why don't you tell me what you've been doing first, okay? Mine may take a while." I knew stalling wouldn't help, but fear had the upper hand.

Denny, who was very slight of build, remained standing in the center of the concrete floor. A wistful smile came upon his face as he shifted his weight from one foot to another.

"Well," he finally blurted out, "you guys probably won't understand this, but . . . last week I accepted Jesus Christ into my life."

"What!" I bellowed with Dennis Marek, bounding up from my chair. "You . . . you're kidding, aren't you? When? Where? How? *Talk,* man!"

Extending both his arms in front of him like a policeman halting traffic, Denny said, "I know you probably think this is crazy, but, honest, last week at a prayer meeting in City Hall in Wickliffe, Ohio, I invited Jesus to come into my heart as my Lord and Savior."

"Denny," I said, putting my hand on his shoulder, "you're never going to believe this, but it happened to me a little over nine months ago, and Dennis here made his decision just a few weeks ago!"

"*What?* What did you just say?"

"That's right!" I exclaimed. "I invited Jesus into my heart at a Pentecostal church service out on the West Side!"

"Did you say Pentecostal, Larry?"

"Yeah, why?"

"Then you've been baptized in the Holy Spirit?"

It was my turn again— "Don't tell me *you* have!"

Denny nodded and began laughing out loud. I started laughing, too.

"*Sshh!*" Dennis said, concerned about the neighbors. Then he, too, succumbed and joined in the celebration.

As our hearts bubbled over with joy, I thought of those first Spirit-filled, on-fire Christians who made such a commotion on Pentecost. We were as excited as little kids on Christmas morning. It was obvious that three "lost souls" had found their way.

Moving into the basement, we spent the next four hours sharing our experiences. Finally, at around four in the morning, Denny Carleton looked me straight in the eye and confronted me. "Larry, are you willing to let the Son of God baptize you in His Holy Spirit—tonight?"

Without hesitating, I said, "I want that more than anything in the world! I've been praying for it almost every day since I accepted Jesus."

Denny said, "All you have to do is make contact with God and let Him know you mean business about a total, unconditional surrender to His will. Give up *all* of yourself to Him. Complete submission . . . a complete dethronement of self to let Jesus Christ become Lord of every part of your life, even your tongue. Then ask Him to fulfill His promise to baptize you in His Spirit." Denny looked at me. "Are you ready to pray right now?"

I nodded slowly. The three of us dropped to our knees on the basement floor. As my two friends placed their hands on my shoulders and began to pray, I prayed as hard as I could and continued in silent devotion, but as so many times before, everything seemed to remain static. The discouragement started to surface, so I repeated my petition, stronger than ever.

"Jesus, You promised that whatever we ask for in Your name

will be ours as long as we believe. I hold You to Your word, Lord, and claim Your promise. Baptize me in Your Holy Spirit, in Your precious name I pray."

My face must have betrayed my emerging dejection, for Denny Carleton's whisper softly penetrated my ear. "Larry, why do you keep on asking? Don't you believe?"

Immediately I froze. Every part of my body locked in place. *Don't you believe?*

All these months I had been asking, backing off, waiting, and then asking again. The words of Jesus came into my mind: "Therefore I tell you, whatever you ask in prayer, *believe* that you receive it, and you will. Without *faith* it is impossible to please God."

As the ice of my doubt began to melt, I became no longer self-conscious but God-conscious.

"Jesus, I have asked, and You promised that I would receive. I claim the promise now. I thank You, Jesus Christ, for baptizing me in Your Holy Spirit! Thank You. Praise Your name."

As thanksgiving and praise erupted from within, a profound sense of God's presence began to well up in me. I felt the rapturous and exultant joy of the Lord surging through me, and the more profuse my praise, the more intense became my desire to magnify the name of my Savior. I grew impatient with the inadequacy of the English language to fully express all that I was feeling, how much I loved God.

Then, just at the right moment, new words began to flow from my heart. At the same time, like a mountain stream— pure, sparkling, cool, crystal clear—living joy began to flow upward and outward through my entire being. It seemed like I was being lifted three feet off the ground.

I could not restrain my tongue, and my lips began to stammer, as a new language hopped, skipped, and somer-saulted from my mouth.

The language was foreign to my ears, a heavenly language

only God could understand. It was praise that had surged through my whole being to seek expression through the Holy Spirit in a new transcendence.

As distant as the echo of an echo was the laughter of my two friends. They were laughing, and I was crying, as I continued to praise God in the new language He had given me.

Finally I lowered my arms and slowly rose to my feet. With my eyes still watering and my nose still running, I turned to Dennis and Denny and hugged them both together in rock-ribbed fashion. *"Hallelujah!"*

Before I knew what was happening, Dennis was on his knees asking Jesus to baptize him in the Holy Spirit, too. No sooner had Denny and I laid our hands on his shoulder and resumed praying than Dennis united his voice with ours in tongues of angelic exaltation.

After a few minutes, I was led to stand perfectly still as my two brothers in Christ continued in prayer. My eyelids remained closed as I stood there, savoring a moment in eternity, a foretaste of heaven. It was a moment outside of time—a moment I would cherish always.

Jesus Christ touched me that night and, oh, the joy that filled my soul! All the uncertainties in my life—the doubts that went along with a faith in God—were erased. I would never feel alone again.

Walking up the basement stairs clutching my Bible, I opened the door and seemed to float through it. Looking up at the cool, crisp, early morning sky, I grinned foolishly, drunk with joy.

CHAPTER

7

OVER six hundred people had turned out for the breakfast meeting in the main ballroom of the Cleveland Statler Hilton to hear Billy Graham announce the plans for his upcoming Cleveland Crusade. Denny Carleton and I had slept less than three hours, yet we had managed to make it in time for the 9:00 A.M. session. Still aglow from my Baptism in the Spirit, just five hours earlier that same morning, I felt no fatigue as I watched Denny make his way toward the speaker's table. Hundreds of people of all ages were packed around the tall, conservatively dressed evangelist whose square-jawed profile was just visible above the crowd.

Normally I would have gone with Denny, but something on my mind demanded immediate reflection. People shuffled by me in the aisle as I propped up my feet on the back of the folding chair in front of me.

What did he mean in his speech, when he referred to an "underground youth movement" in the Church today? And what in heaven's name is a "Jesus revolution"?

Revolution was a term often heard at anti-war rallies and demonstrations; in a Christian context, it seemed decidedly out of place.

"Maybe," I said to no one in particular, "a revolution is just what we need. Just think what would happen if God lit a spark among young people to bring back the Gospel into the

Church! Imagine a whole army of former radicals, addicts, and amoralists declaring their allegiance to Jesus and admitting they were wrong in turning off God because of churchianity! That would shake this country up a little! What would the religious hierarchy do? It would blow their minds!"

As I chuckled at my daydream, I got up and headed for the exit. Denny was getting a ride home with some other friends. I had plans to visit somebody whom I had not seen in years, someone whose name had suddenly come to me before I got out of bed that morning.

"Father Sommer!" I shouted as the door opened and I beheld the smiling countenance of my six-foot friend. His hair was a little grayer, but his boyish permanent-press grin hadn't changed.

"Larry Tomczak! Come in. Talk about surprises!"

No sooner had I sat down than I had to tell him: "Father Sommer, I've found Jesus! And just this morning He baptized me in His Holy Spirit!"

As his eyebrows raised wrinkles on his forehead, Father muttered, "What?"

"Yes, it happened at 4:00 A.M., with Denny Carleton and Dennis Marek. Just like you told me happened at Notre Dame three years ago."

"Glory to God!" Shaking his head in gleeful disbelief, Father sat back in his chair and asked me to start at the beginning.

And so for the next half hour I retraced the last three years. At times he laughed heartily; other times, his expression conveyed a deep sadness as I told him about the situation at home and at Holy Cross Church.

"Larry," he said, "I know what it's like at Holy Cross. Every so often I celebrate Mass there, and sometimes I wonder if everyone has fallen asleep. But it's not just at Holy Cross, I'm afraid."

"Father, do you have any idea how bitter college kids are toward God and Church? And how many profess to be

atheists, especially among Catholics?" Springing from my seat,
I threw up my arms and asked, "Father Sommer, what are we
doing to do to reach out to the millions and millions of young
people who've fallen away? How are we ever going to get
them back into the Church?"

Father Sommer remained seated.

"Larry, I don't try to get them back into the Church."

"Huh?"

"I try to bring them to Jesus first. Without Him, everything
is just formalism anyway. There's too much of that already.
What you and I have to do is go out into the world and fulfill
the commission that Jesus Himself gave us: 'Go and preach the
Gospel to every creature.' They'll listen—if we approach them
in humility and meekness, trusting the Spirit for the right
words and leading, and giving them the Lord's love and
compassion."

I sat down and calmed down.

"Larry," Father continued, "the Bible says that 'God is not
mocked,' and He's not. He has work to be done, and right now
we're the only mouthpiece He has. That's why He baptized us
in His Holy Spirit. He's given us the power to be His witnesses.
But we're not alone. Remember how I told you that Pentecost
was not over—that it's happening today in the Catholic
church?"

"Sure, that's why I'm here right now."

"Larry, Pentecost was only a few drops of the coming
shower. What we're now experiencing is the beginning of the
fulfillment of Joel's prophecy: 'In the last days it shall be, God
declares, that I will pour out my Spirit upon all flesh.'

"All over the world, a tidal wave of spiritual revival and
renewal is touching the nations, transforming the lives of
hundreds of thousands. Prayer meetings are springing up
simultaneously in every city and town I know of; home
Bible-study groups are spreading like wild-fire; personal wit-

nessing and prayer have become for many as natural as breathing."

"Praise God!" I exclaimed. "And I thought I was going to be a Catholic loner in this Christian walk."

"*Loner?*" Father Sommer retorted. "Larry, do you realize that since my experience at Notre Dame, the Pentecostal movement in the Catholic church has swollen from a relative handful of people to roughly a hundred thousand Catholics!"

"*What!* In the . . . the Catholic church?"

"Sure! We've all got the head knowledge—now we're learning what it means to take Jesus out of our head and allow Him to come into our heart. That spells commitment. And it's happening everywhere."

Closing my eyes for a few seconds, I shook my head, utterly dumbfounded. Everything seemed to be spinning around in a whirlpool—a spiritual whirlpool that seemed to be drawing together the people of God—the people who were willing and eager to serve Jesus, in any way that He called them.

"Larry," Father said, "something so enormous is beginning to happen that we can't even imagine it, and you and I are privileged to be a part of it."

"Amen."

As I apologized for taking up so much time, he put his hand on my arm. "Just one thing, though, before you go. It's something that I was going to tell you earlier, but I'm glad I waited till now so we can pray together about it."

"What's that, Father?"

"Larry, when you go back to Cleveland State, you'll have company: I've been assigned to be a chaplain at CSU during the coming year."

My first reaction was to jump for joy, but the imposing responsibility held me back. Without saying a word, Father Sommer and I bowed our heads in prayer—for each other, the University, the Church, and the ministry that God had carved out for our lives.

When I arrived home for supper, I could not contain my
enthusiasm about the events of the past twenty-four hours,
which further alienated my parents, though they were at a loss
for words over what I told them about Father Sommer and the
Pentecostal movement in the Catholic church. Both of them
respected and trusted Father Sommer; they knew him well.
"What is happening to our Church?" Mom kept saying.
"What's going on?"

To my amazement, the reaction of my sister was appreciably
different. For the first time in nine months, Margaret was
actually interested. The interest was aloof and skeptical, but it
was there.

That Saturday evening the Christians at Bethel Temple
were having a fellowship supper on the grounds behind the
church. There was to be no formal service, only a time of
community sharing. The entire evening was made for my
sister. Having put on eighty pounds since her broken romance,
Margaret had stopped counting calories. The prospect of all
that free food was too much for her to resist.

"All right, all right!" she said. "I'll come to that silly church,
and once and for all I'm going to find out what the whole
thing's about!"

So on Saturday, at five o'clock, Margaret and I pulled out of
our driveway for the forty-minute trip to the church. Wearing
her habitual sour expression and speaking in the abrasive
manner that had become a part of her personality, Margaret
sat puffing her menthol cigarettes and reviewing some regi-
mental instructions while I drove.

"Now, remember," Margaret said, "one hour. And not a
minute longer! One hour!"

"Yes, Margaret."

"And I'm not staying for any kind of church service!"

"Right, Margaret."

"And don't try to get me to sing any songs, either. I don't
feel like singing!"

I nodded.

"And nobody better start preaching at me at this thing."

"Okay."

Stubbing out her cigarette in the ashtray, Margaret flicked on the car radio and punched button after button in search of a song to suit her taste.

"Could you turn it down a little?"

"What for?" she said. "I like music!"

"So do I, but not blaring. Please?"

"Turn it off then, damn it!" Margaret shouted as she snapped off the music and sat back in a huff.

I started to rise up then but caught myself in the nick of time. *Jesus, help me! Grant me Your peace in abundance right now. Change my heart, and give me Your love for Margaret. And, Lord, touch her heart and soften it, that she may begin to know how much You love her.*

A peace settled over me so profound that I had to be careful not to grin for joy. After a few minutes of silence, Margaret put forth a question as she lit another cigarette.

"What the hell are these people giving me free food for? Are you sure I don't have to pay?"

"No, you don't have to pay anything, Margaret. They're just sharing the way early Christians did, like it says in the Book of Acts."

"Now don't get started on the Bible, see?"

"Sorry."

But incredibly, I seemed to be getting a green light from the Lord. Slowly, gently, praying for just the right words from the Spirit, I pursued the point.

"Margaret, did you know that what many people think of as Christianity is not Christianity at all?"

"What do you mean?"

"Well, most of us have never really seen Jesus Christ in the Church today."

"Seen Him?"

"Well, not physically . . . but we've never really seen Him manifested in the lives of the believers."

"How's that?" asked Margaret.

"Look at what Jesus said to believers, and be honest. Ask yourself if we see this in the Church today: Jesus said, 'Seek the low places not the high.' He said, 'If someone slaps you on the cheek, turn to him the other . . . if someone needs your coat, let him have your cloak as well . . . if someone begs from you, give him what he needs and don't ask in return.' . . . He instructed us to love our enemies, bless those who persecute us, and pray for those who despitefully use us. Do we see this in the Church today?"

"Are you kidding? It's just the opposite," Margaret answered.

"Right! Why? Because Christianity is a battle not a dream. Authentic Christianity rubs people the wrong way. And what are we seeing in its place? Churchianity. You know, go to church for an hour on Sunday and say, 'I'm a Christian.' But that's not what Jesus said. He said, 'If you want to come after me, take up your cross *daily* and follow me.' Every day. Twenty-four hours."

My sister flicked her cigarette out the window. She didn't say anything, but I knew God had her attention.

"Margaret, if you only knew how much love He has been waiting to give you . . ."

"But I've tried. I've gone to church all my life."

Margaret was finally coming alive. *Jesus, help me. Help us both!*

"So did I, Margaret, but churchgoing won't necessarily provide the answer! Think of it this way— God created man and gave him a wonderful, abundant life. In the beginning, God and man were in perfect fellowship. But for the sake of real fellowship, God created man with a free will. And what happened? Man chose to disobey God; the result was a separation.

"Man has tried many ways to bridge the gap and get back to God—by good works, philosophy, ethics, religion—but to no avail. So what did God do? He bridged the gap by sending His Son, Jesus Christ, to *save* us from eternal separation by His death on the cross. He paid the full penalty for all our sins. Jesus took our sin, our death, our judgment, and our own place on the cross.

"A lot of people say to me, 'So when were you saved?' I always tell them, 'Two thousand years ago. But I didn't accept it until December of last year!' "

"I know all that from grade school," Margaret replied. "Everyone knows that Christ died for our sins."

"Yeah, so did I, Marg, but head knowledge isn't enough."

"What do you mean?" She looked bewildered.

"Because there are *three* doors down inside every one of us. One is intellect, another is emotion, and a third is will. Intellectually, you may accept Christ. Emotionally, you may feel that you love Him. However, until you have surrendered to Christ by a definite act of your will, you are not a Christian.

"Jesus wants to enter your life, but He won't barge in. You've got to invite Him."

"But, Larry, if Christ died for us, we must be saved automatically, right?"

"No," I quickly responded, "that's not what God says. He says there is salvation for all, but not that all are saved. Look: Suppose it's a bitterly cold winter in Cleveland this year and unemployment is critical. So City Hall provides free meals. Now one day you meet a poor fellow downtown who says he is starving. Naturally you ask if he hasn't seen the notices that are up all over the city, that there is enough food for all provided free.

" 'Oh, yes,' he replies, 'I've seen them, and believe they are true in a general sort of way, but I am still hungry.'

"You know what you'd do? You'd tell him that he is likely to remain hungry in spite of the provisions unless he bothers to eat and drink personally of what is provided for all.

"So, although the death of Christ provided salvation for whosoever will, only those are *saved* who personally accept Christ and believe that He died in their place."

As my sister listened, I began to sense a stirring of the real Margaret Tomczak again—the sister that I once knew. But just as my hopes began to soar, she realized that she had allowed her mask to slip.

"Look, damn it, I didn't come along to be preached at! Understand?"

"Okay, okay . . . take it easy—I'm sorry!" *But praise You, Lord, that she heard as much as she did!*

The hour spent at the fellowship supper was beyond my most tremulous hopes. The way the Holy Spirit orchestrated each meeting, cued each conversation, and conducted the timing of each sequence—it was as if He was demonstrating to me just how much could be accomplished in an hour, *if* I left it all to Him.

The Christians from the church opened their hearts to Margaret and made her feel so completely at ease that even her callous attitude seemed to melt under the power of His love.

When it came time for the two of us to make our pre-arranged exit, I noticed Margaret surrounded by a large group of people. As they hugged my sister, several times I heard, "See you tomorrow night at the service, Margaret!"

Lord, keep me from going into orbit!

The wall that my sister had built around herself was crumbling before my eyes. Caught in a sea of liquid love, she was helpless.

"Understand, Larry," she said to me on the way home, "I'm only going as an observer—just an observer—that's all."

"Right, Margaret, just an observer."

It was a few minutes past seven when Margaret and I walked through the back doors of Bethel Temple the next night.

On the platform was Pastor Davidson, and seated alongside him was a short handsome man with a receding hairline who looked about forty years old. He was Coleman McDuff, the guest evangelist for the night.

"Oh, Jesus," I prayed silently as we sat down, "may Your holy perfect will be done in Margaret's heart tonight. Complete the work You've begun in her. In Your name I pray."

The first forty-five minutes of the service was a time of worship of God—jubilant songs of praise, adoration, and thanksgiving were sung as the congregation clapped their hands; testimonies were given spontaneously as people shared recent experiences in their Christian life; and a time of open prayer was set aside for uplifting the various needs of the community.

A tremendous joyfulness pervaded the tone and the spirit of the service. When we took time to greet each other with a handshake or a hug, the undercurrent of joy bubbled to the surface. Any anxiety that Margaret might have brought into the church was quickly dispelled by the openness and freedom that prevailed. In fact, my sister was returning smile for smile!

The last half of the evening was devoted to the evangelist. As he spoke, I was in prayer for the Holy Spirit to bring my sister under conviction to make her decision for Jesus Christ.

Coleman McDuff concluded his message by moving away from the pulpit and speaking in a very soft voice: "I'm going to ask that everyone in this church come forward and stand around the front of this platform united in prayer. I'd like to ask all of you right now to get up out of your seats and move forward as we all sing, 'How Great Thou Art.' "

The organ began to play as people all over the church rose up, began singing, and started streaming into the aisles.

Margaret clutched my arm as I stood. "Larry?" she said in perplexity. "What . . ."

Before my sister knew what was happening, she was caught in the current. Up from her seat, into the aisle, moving forward, Margaret was on her way.

In minutes, the entire congregation was assembled shoulder-to-shoulder around the front platform, and the singing came to a halt. Margaret stood quietly at my side, and for the first time that evening, I could hear her whispering a prayer.

As a tone of rest—of resting in God—flooded the atmosphere, a gentle murmur of prayer from the congregation became audible. Joining the rest of the people, I bowed my head and entered into communion with my Creator.

All of a sudden I heard a compassionate voice coming from someone between Margaret and me.

"What's wrong, sister?"

Lifting my head, I saw that God had directed evangelist McDuff straight to my sister. He stood beside her, his right arm resting across her shoulder.

Margaret's eyes were closed, and her head remained lowered. I could see that her lips were quivering.

A gentle smile came upon the evangelist's face, and he leaned forward, saying, "Sister, you don't have to go on anymore with that burden you're carrying. Let Christ come in by His Spirit and set you free."

As he finished, Margaret slowly raised her head. Her eyelids were closed, her lips pressed firmly together; flinching slightly, she began to shake her head from side to side. Finally, she could hold back the tears no longer.

Coleman rested my sister's head on his chest as she vented the bitterness that he had been accumulating for so long in the recesses of her heart.

Finally, in childlike simplicity, Margaret began, "Jesus . . . I'm . . . I'm sorry for my sins. I need You, Jesus Christ, and I need You right now. Please help me . . . I accept You as my Lord and Savior. Come into my life and make me the kind of person You want me to be."

I stood there motionless and began to cry.

Margaret's prayer moved all of heaven and created a stir that reverberated even to the little white house on East 200th Street.

"You did *what?*" Mom and Dad said as Margaret stood in the center of the living room and told them what had happened.

Flicking off the Sunday night movie that was still in progress, my parents sat side by side on the couch, trying with every fiber of their being to understand what Margaret's experience was all about.

Sitting on the steps that led to my sister's bedroom, I flipped through my Bible, chuckling to myself as I listened in on the proceedings, and asking the Lord to help her with the right words.

Because of Margaret's hitherto despondent state of mind, Mom and Dad were more receptive to her disclosure than they had been to mine, conveying a general "well-anything-that-will-make-you-happy-is-fine-with-us" attitude.

When Margaret finished, Mom took a sip of her coffee and issued a warning—

"Whatever you and Larry do now with your lives is up to you; you're both adults. But as long as you're in *our* house, you'll do as your father and I say. If you don't like it—there's the door.

"Now let me make two points crystal clear: You just leave your father and me alone about this religion you're into; and also, I don't want either of you mentioning any of this stuff to my family. Understand?"

"But Jesus told us that we have to be witnesses!" Margaret replied. "He doesn't—"

"Listen, young lady, I don't want the relatives involved in any of this! They already know enough of our problems. What would they think of us if they heard about this?"

In a soft, sincere tone of voice that I had not heard her use in years, Margaret replied, "What is more important to you, Mom—our reputation in the eyes of your two sisters and your brother, or our obedience to the commandment of Jesus?"

Dad, who had been unusually silent throughout, looked at Mom for her answer.

Finishing her coffee, Mother finally gave her response, pausing deliberately after each word.

"Just . . . leave . . . my . . . family . . . out . . . of . . . it!"

The next few months until Christmas were a time of more change in our family. The arguments were still there, but they were diminishing in intensity and frequency. Tension no longer had its vise-like grip on our home.

Christ's mysterious healing power was progressively manifested in Margaret's life. Although it was not immediate, as she exposed herself more and more to God's Word in Bible study, prayer meetings, and fellowship with other Christians, Margaret's heart of stone began to soften. The Holy Spirit was bringing powerful conviction upon various areas of her life, and with God's grace, significant progress was being made.

The most important evidence of the "new creation" that Christ was fashioning was Margaret's temperament. The cynical, argumentative, abrasive shell was giving way, and with it went the liquor, the cigarettes, the profanity, and the gluttony. Instead, the Lord was planting seeds of patience, gentleness, goodness, and self-control.

Dad, whose own volatile nature had always plagued him, was most perceptive of the new Margaret. On numerous occasions, he even made a few complimentary remarks to her.

Mother remained the most distant. Whenever a discussion

began to move toward the spiritual, she changed the subject. In periods of frustration, she often said to both Margaret and me, "Why, oh why, do you kids have to be so different?"

As for me, the Lord was doing His best to work peace and patience in me, and though at times I seemed to be doing my best to hinder Him, it was beginning to bear fruit in my academic work and my responsibilities as student body president. As I slowly learned to let the Lord do it, I was getting twice as much done, with half the effort. In fact, I could actually relax and *enjoy* what I was doing.

Working jointly with Father Sommer and an expanding number of young Catholics who had made their decisions for Christ, we inaugurated a two-hour weekly prayer meeting on the CSU campus, bringing the good news of Jesus Christ to the student body. Meeting in a classroom, our group grew from nine students to forty in just a few weeks.

On the first day of 1971, I made a resolution that I would repeat each morning of the new year: to make optimum utilization of all my time and talents for the kingdom of God.

The first idea that God brought to mind concerned a way of reaching out to the Catholic families in the Cleveland metropolitan area. What better way, I thought, than to go directly through the official Catholic diocesan newspaper.

Sitting down one Sunday night in mid-January, I wrote an article delineating my experience with Christ for the *Catholic Universe Bulletin*.

"Jesus," I prayed as I put the testimony in an envelope, "make use of this for the greater honor and glory of Your name. If it be Your will, honor this effort."

The very next Friday afternoon, I opened the *Universe Bulletin*, and there, emblazoned across the top of the front page, was my picture and the headline: "LET'S RAP ABOUT THE FAITH, SAYS CSU STUDENT BODY PRESIDENT."

More than eighty thousand Catholic families in the Cleveland area read the story, and things started to happen. The editors got such enthusiastic response to the article that they asked me if I would coordinate a weekly series in the paper, featuring other such "unique" testimonies of young Catholics who had found Christ.

Catholic newspapers in other cities and states ran the article. Scores of letters and phone calls came from Catholic parents who begged me to pray for their sons and daughters who "wanted nothing more to do with the Church"; young high school and college students who "identified with all of my feelings, but couldn't quite understand what 'accepting Christ' really meant," and nuns and priests who were frustrated in trying to teach religion to their students asked if I'd "please come and speak at a school assembly."

With every letter, phone call, and personal contact that came my way, I sensed a terrible despondency. Some of the parents and religious were on the verge of tears. The experiences they shared with me concerning the young people under them made me more aware than ever of how acutely critical the situation was. And everything I heard seemed to be a re-play of my own experience.

Now the Lord began opening doors for speaking engagements in Catholic grade schools, high schools, assemblies, youth retreats, and confraternity classes throughout the Greater Cleveland area. Denny Carleton and other Catholic friends who had found the Lord often accompanied me and shared a testimony in word or song. And before long, in response to the series in the *Catholic Universe Bulletin*, I started receiving letters from other young Catholics who said they "accepted Christ at a Catholic Pentecostal prayer meeting or a Bible study and wanted to help spread the good news."

During the first three months of 1971, God arranged two other opportunities to reach more people for the cause of Christ.

First, I was appointed to serve as the first student member

on the Cleveland State University Board of Trustees. Then,
Cleveland Mayor Carl B. Stokes appointed me to serve a
four-year term on the city's Community Relations Board. With
both these positions came major newspaper and radio inter-
views in which I was able to share testimony and give the glory
to Jesus.

I particularly remember sitting down at the cluttered desk
of a middle-aged newspaper reporter from the Cleveland *Press*
who quickly loosened his tie, pulled a pencil from behind his
ear, slapped his notebook down on his desk, and posed his
question in a very straightforward, authoritative tone:

"So, how does it feel to be the youngest person in
Cleveland's history appointed to serve in city government?"

As the reporter readied his pencil, I blinked a few times and
then replied, "Well, you see, I owe it all to the fact that I
accepted Jesus Christ as my Lord and Savior."

Thud!

The reporter slowly lifted his head.

"Huh?"

Grinning, I repeated my answer.

"I said, I owe it all to the fact that I accepted Jesus Christ as
my Lord and Savior."

"Oh."

He wrinkled his forehead and wrote down my response,
muttering to himself, "I owe it all . . . to the fact . . . that
. . . I . . . *cough-cough* . . . accepted . . . *cough* . . . Jesus
Christ into my life . . . as my Lord . . . and Savior. Is that
right?"

"Yep!"

By mid-March, I was becoming increasingly interested in
the Pentecostal movement in the Catholic church. The
outpouring of the Holy Spirit was so pronounced that even
ultra-conservative Catholic theologians were taking notice,
and in Cleveland, five major prayer groups were meeting
weekly in Catholic high schools and college auditoriums

throughout the city. At my former high school, Saint Joe's, the Tuesday night prayer meeting was now drawing between five and six hundred people, at least a third of which were under twenty-five. Each week I met numbers of young Catholics, formerly turned off to the Church, who had now discovered the reality of Jesus Christ through one of the area prayer groups. Many told me that they made their decision for Christ at the Saint Joe's meeting, which always closed with an invitation for people to stand and accept Christ as Lord and Savior.

The prayer meetings were interdenominational gatherings where Christians could read Scripture, pray, sing, clap their hands, and share a "word of testimony"—all under the direction and in the unity of the Spirit.

My second time at the prayer meeting at Saint Joe's, a priest, two nuns, and fifteen other people prayed with me for a healing of an acute facial dermatitis that had plagued me for over three years. It had required bimonthly check-ups with a specialist at the Cleveland Clinic, as well as a morning-evening application of a cortisone prescription each day. If I failed to apply the cortisone ointment, the affected area would seriously inflame and blister.

As I was sitting in a prayer room at Saint Joe's with the Spirit-filled believers gathered around me, a priest named Father Phil invoked the promise of Jesus. "If two of you agree on earth about anything they ask, it will be done for them by my Father in heaven. For where two or three are gathered in my name, there am I in the midst of them." Claiming the healing, I left the meeting, thanking Jesus for what He had done.

That night when the temptation came to apply the cortisone, the Lord's words came to mind: "Therefore, I tell you, whatever you ask in prayer, *believe* that you receive it, and you will."

Knowing that the Bible said, "Without *faith*, it is impossible to please God," I left the ointment in the medicine cabinet and spent as much time as possible reading the Holy Bible.

Within three days my seborrheic dermatitis was completely gone.

"Praise the Lord!" I shouted, as I looked at the smooth, clear complexion in the bathroom mirror that Saturday morning. "He *healed* me!" I ran out of the bathroom into the kitchen, still in my underwear.

Mom and Dad, in their pajamas, were sitting at the table munching hot buttered toast. Dad's fuzzy face grew pale—he knew what had happened. Three days previously, I had shared with him my expectation for the healing.

"Look! *Look!*" I said frantically, leaning over the kitchen table and almost spilling Mom's cup of coffee. "Check out what God can do!"

Mom and Dad were dumbstruck—they remained absolutely silent. Then Dad began to speak to Mom in Polish, and I backed quietly out of the kitchen, went to my room and began to pray.

8

"DAD, if I told you I was going to become a priest, what would you say?"

"Huh?"

"Come on, what would you say?"

"Well, you're old enough now to decide what's best for your life. If that's what you want, go right ahead."

"You think I'd ever make it to the Vatican? Could you picture me as Pope? Pope Larry the First!"

Dad and I both laughed heartily. Having finished supper early, Dad and I sat in the living room spooning the last of man-sized portions of mint chocolate-chip ice cream. Mom and Margaret were out shopping for some Easter clothes, and the two of us were home alone.

Almost two weeks had gone by since the Saturday "kitchen incident." Each day my prayer had been to wait on the Lord for His perfect timing; I had promised Him that I would curb all witnessing to Mom and Dad until He gave me an unmistakable green light.

When the phone rang during supper confirming cancellation of a meeting I was planning to attend, I knew that the Lord had circumstances under control. "Jesus," I whispered in hanging up the receiver, "help me to stay completely out of Your way and speak only what You give me to say. In Your name I pray. Amen."

Dad was sitting in the corner of the couch with his right leg stretched across one of the cushions. On his lap was the bowl of ice cream. He was in an unusually good mood, even poking fun at himself when a few drops of ice cream landed on his shirt.

As Dad finished his ice cream, he put the bowl on the floor. Sitting back in his seat, he stretched his arms behind his head, yawned, and then said, "Why don't you turn on the TV? What's on now, anyway?"

"Uh, the news won't be on for another hour," I replied. "There's nothing good now—okay if we leave it off?"

"Fine with me."

The time had come; if I did not strike up a conversation immediately, Dad would just lie back and take a nap.

"Ah . . . Dad . . . can we talk for a bit?"

"What about?" he answered, stifling a second yawn.

"Well . . . ah . . ."

But before I even got started, Dad anticipated me. "Larry, can't you talk about anything but church?"

I leaned forward in the armchair, propped my elbows on my knees, and said, "Dad, if I promise that I won't talk about 'church,' could the two of us engage in a man-to-man talk with each other? I don't think we've ever done that. What do you say?"

"Why not? What do you want to talk about?"

Reaching for my Bible on the table, I picked it up and gently flipped it over to Dad. He caught it and held it in his hands.

"Big book, isn't it?" I began. "There are more than seven hundred thousand words between those two covers."

"That many?"

"Yep! But you know, the whole reason why it was written is contained in one sentence in the first letter of John. Want to guess what that is?"

Dad chuckled. "Larry, you know I don't read the Bible.

What do you say we talk about something else? Like what's going on at college, or what you're going to do when you graduate.

"All right, all right," Dad retorted, seeing my face. "I'll bite. What's the reason? Why was the Bible written?"

I took the Bible back from him and turned to I John. "These things I am writing to you that you may know that you have eternal life—you who believe in the name of the Son of God" (I John 5:13, Conf. Version).

"Let me see that." Dad reached for the Bible. He focused on the verse I had underlined in red.

"Hey! You're right! It does say that!"

"Let me ask you another question," I began. "Dad, suppose that you were to die tonight and stand before God, and He were to ask you, 'Why should I let you into heaven?' what would you reply?"

Dad mused over the question for a few moments and then said, "Well, I've tried to be a good Catholic . . . lead a decent life and obey the Ten Commandments. I've never intentionally missed Mass. I don't think I've been too bad."

"Anything else?"

"I've been an usher for a number of years and helped out in a lot of parish projects. I've always given my Sunday offerings, too!"

"So you'd say to God: 'I've been a good Catholic, led a decent life, obeyed the Commandments, attended Mass, served as an usher, helped out in the parish, and faithfully given a weekly offering,' right?"

"Right."

"Dad, I've got some good news for you! Heaven is not something a person earns, or deserves, or works for. According to the Bible, heaven—eternal life—is an absolutely free gift."

"A free gift?"

"Yep, the Bible says that eternal life is a free gift, unearned, unworked for, and undeserved. Free!"

"Oh, go on, nothing's free!"

I sat down next to him on the couch. Opening the Bible to Romans 6:23, I pointed to the verse so that Dad could read for himself.

"For the wages of sin is death, but the gift of God is life everlasting in Christ Jesus our Lord" (Conf. Version).

"Hey!" Dad exclaimed. "I never knew that!"

"Dad, when the Gospel is read at Mass, do you remember hearing the words of Jesus, 'How narrow the gate and close the way that leads to life! And few there are who find it' ? " (Matt. 7:14 Conf. Version).

"Sure."

"Well, if only a few find this gift of eternal life, wouldn't you like to be one of them?"

"Of course!"

"The first thing we want to look at is what God says about man." Flipping the pages of the Bible, I found Romans 3:23 for Dad to read: "all have sinned and have need of the glory of God."

Dad looked up from the page. "So what's new about that? In the Mass we say, 'I confess to almighty God . . . that I have sinned through my fault.' I know that everyone is a sinner."

"Well, because man is a sinner, and a sinner can do no good thing of himself anyway, it is impossible for him to earn his way into heaven, even if it weren't free, which we've just seen that it is. The Bible states this very clearly: "For by grace you have been saved through faith; and that not from yourselves, for it is gift of God; not as the outcome of works, lest anyone may boast (Eph. 2:8–9, Conf. Version).

"Hold on a second," Dad said. "Let me read that last one again!" His face appeared slightly pale.

"Larry," he finally said, "I want to receive this gift of eternal life. What do I do?"

"See, Dad," I said, "*faith* is the key that opens the door to eternal life. Do you fully understand what the Bible means here by 'faith' ? "

"Well, I have faith. I believe in God."

"Sure you do. Here, Dad, read this," I said, pointing to the open Bible. "Thou believest that there is one God. Thou dost well. The devils also believe, and tremble" (James 2:19 Conf. Version).

"I never saw that!" my father exclaimed.

"See, Dad, we're talking about 'saving faith' and not just an intellectual assent to certain historical facts—"

"Now just a minute," Dad interrupted, "I do more than just assent. I pray every morning and every night. I ask God to help us pay the bills, keep us all alive and well. He answers my prayers, too!" he continued.

"It's good to pray, Dad, and to trust God for these things, but that's still not saving faith."

"What do you mean?" he demanded, his face turning red.

"When you trust the Lord to take care of our family," I explained, "that we might call family-faith. When you trust Him to help you pay the bills? Well, that might be called financial-faith. But do you notice one element both these things have in common?"

Dad thought for a few seconds and then just shrugged his shoulders.

"Dad, all these things are temporary—they'll all pass away one day."

"Okay, I see that. But what is this saving faith?"

"Saving faith is trusting Jesus Christ to save you forever, eternally, no matter what else may happen. For years I was trusting God for one thing after another—just like you, Dad. I thought trusting and praying here on earth would please Him so that He would give me eternal salvation some day. I tried to be a faithful church member. I tried to live a decent life. I tried to obey the Ten Commandments. I, I, I, I. *I* was really trying to be my own savior."

Dad's face lit up like a lightbulb.

Pointing into the dining room, I said, "See that chair over there? Do you believe that chair exists?"

"Of course," said Dad.

"Do you believe that it would hold you up?"

"Sure, but . . ."

"But it's not holding you up," I continued, "because you're not sitting on it. And that's the way it is right now with you and Jesus Christ. You believe Jesus exists. You believe He is God, and you trust Him for many things in your life. But as far as your eternal welfare is concerned, you have been trusting in your own efforts to please God.

"Suppose this couch you're sitting on represents all the good works you've been counting on for eternal life. And suppose that dining-room chair represents Jesus Christ and what He did for you on the cross. You could transfer your trust from this couch to that dining room chair by getting up and going over to sit in that chair. Then no longer would you be resting on this couch of good works, you'd be resting on one thing—"

"Jesus Christ!" Dad exploded.

"That's right. So you don't have to do anything," I concluded, "but start resting on what He has done for you, just as I did a little over a year ago. I transferred my trust from myself—from what I could do—to Jesus Christ and what He had done already. I accepted His gift of eternal life."

Dad slumped back on the couch. Shaking his head back and forth, he said, "Whew! Sixty years . . . sixty years . . . not aware . . . trying to do it myself, when He had done it already."

As my father bowed his head, I knelt down in front of him and began to read— "For if thou confess with thy mouth that Jesus is the Lord, and believe in thy heart that God has raised him from the dead, thou shalt be saved: (Rom. 10:9 Conf. Version).

As I led in the prayer, Dad began to repeat each phrase after me.

"Jesus Christ, I admit that I've sinned against You. I'm sorry for my sins. I believe that You are the Son of God. I believe that You died for my sins, and I accept Your forgiveness for them. Lord, I have been trusting myself and my own good works. Now I put my trust in You. I openly receive You as my personal Savior. And I confess You as my Lord. I invite You into my life right now. I accept Your gift of eternal life. In Your name I pray. Amen."

Immediately I threw my arms around Dad's neck, "Thank You, Jesus!" I shouted.

Dad just laughed and shook his head.

I picked up my Bible which had fallen on the floor and opened to one final verse.

"Here Dad, read this verse and delight in the promise of Jesus: 'Amen, amen, I say to you, he who believes in me has life everlasting!' (John 6:47 Conf. Version).

As my father finished, he looked up with a glow radiating from his face. I could almost hear the angels singing!

Dad stood and tucked the Bible under his arm. Still shaking his head, he sighed, and then chuckled. "Praise the Lord, son."

Poor Mom was now fighting an uphill battle against God and the three people she loved the most.

Her initial reaction to my father's experience—"Stanley, you *what?*"—gradually began to wane after we persuaded her to attend one of the Catholic charismatic prayer meetings at Saint Joe's. Mom, whose respect and strong affinity for nuns dated back to her early years at Holy Cross convent, was impressed by the number of Sisters at the meeting.

Then the prayer-meeting leader came over, and she was really undone. It was Father Sommer, one of Mom's favorite priests!

"Well, praise the Lord, Mrs. Tomczak!" Father Sommer said upon seeing her.

Clearing her throat and straightening her glasses, Mother managed a garbled, "Good evening, Father."

Even though Mom constantly reminded the three of us to just leave her alone, her interest in spiritual concerns was growing, and her attempts to conceal it were not always successful. On numerous occasions I caught her flipping through my Bible or reading articles on the Catholic Pentecostal movement in our *Catholic Universe Bulletin*. By mid-May, she was a regular attender at the Saint Joe's prayer meeting. Meanwhile, Margaret and Dad, once bitter antagonists, were being drawn closer together in the love of Christ. Praying for each other and sharing Scripture were not the only things that the Lord was using to heal old hurts. At least once or twice a month, after Sunday Mass, Dad and Margaret jumped into my sister's car and went for a drive to the country. As they backed out of the driveway, Mom usually stood at the front window waving goodbye, a pensive expression on her face.

As my college career drew to a close, I found myself embroiled in so many activities that solitary moments were at a premium. My hours of sleep were diminishing with each passing week, and Mother was becoming increasingly concerned about my health. It wasn't until I fell asleep during a major board meeting at Cleveland City Hall that I finally decided I'd better slow down.

At CSU the prayer meetings were blossoming in attendance and in depth of worship. In addition, I began to meet one evening a week for special "growth" sessions with nine Catholic Pentecostal friends from the University.

The main topic of discussion at these meetings was the possibility of committing ourselves, full-time, to a Christian community household near the campus. The spiritual vacuum of the student body, the drug problem, and numerous other factors were making the establishment of such a household an absolute necessity.

Doors that Christ opened for me to communicate the Gospel increased weekly: speaking opportunities at Catholic high school assemblies; working with priests and nuns on retreats to motivate adolescents into a personal relationship with Christ; joining Father Sommer for speaking engagements in various Midwestern cities as well as parts of Canada; being interviewed on radio programs and giving my witness for Christ.

The three-month period prior to my graduation from Cleveland State University was the busiest and most rewarding time of my life. My New Year's Day pledge to make the optimum utilization of all my time and talents for the kingdom of God brought me blessings far beyond my expectations.

Suddenly it was June 13, 1971—Graduation Day at Cleveland State University. Garbed in cap and gown, I sat on the speakers' platform between the other members of the Board of Trustees and the President of the University. Somewhat nervous, I tapped my foot and scanned the capacity crowd squeezed into the ten-thousand-seat auditorium. Thousands of excited parents, grandparents, brothers, sisters, relatives, and friends were on hand for the commencement exercises. I could almost hear the throbbing hearts reverberating as flashbulbs popped throughout the auditorium.

Mom and Dad were sitting alongside Margaret in the upper balcony. Seeing them, I grinned and almost waved. "Thanks, Dad and Mom. Thanks for everything," I whispered.   '

My parents were bursting with pride. All their sacrificing— the floor-scrubbing, the window-washing, the walking to work, the physical suffering—flashed across my mind, and I prayed that the Lord would reward them this day, as I never could.

He did, and rewarded me as well, with unexpected honors. First, special recognition was given for *cum laude* academic achievement. Mother barely had her teardrops dried when two other honors were bestowed—the Cleveland State University "President's Award" and the "Senior of the Year Award."

"The glory is all Yours, Lord," was all I could think.

Later in the day, all the relatives came by the house for a graduation party. In the middle of the living room, Dad put a table for displaying my diploma, collegiate photograph, certificates of merit, and the two framed awards that I had received. Most surprising, though, to my relatives was what occupied the central position on the table. It was my graduation present from my parents—a big, black, beautiful Bible!

Gold-stamped, leather-bound, bold-printed, it was breathtaking! So were the reactions of my relatives who came upon it.

"What's that?"

"A Bible?"

"Huh?"

"Oh, how nice."

Throughout the afternoon, one question was consistently put forth by the parade of well-wishers who stopped by the house. It was a question I had been confronted with as long as I could remember. Only now when someone inquired, "So Larry, what are you going to do with your life?" I was able to say,

"Uncle Ken . . .

Uncle Bob . . .

Aunt Irene . . .

Aunt Al . . .

Aunt June . . .

Aunt Stella . . .

Aunt Noreen . . .

Uncle Jack . . .

Jesus Christ has arranged a position for me!"

My relatives, whom I loved very much, were then let in on the secret.

"Next month I'm leaving Cleveland, Ohio, and moving to Washington, D.C. Six months ago a man who helped lead me to Jesus Christ, Mel Witt, one of the city's key labor leaders, informed me of a position that would be vacant in July 1971 at the National Headquarters of the AFL-CIO, directly across from the White House. He urged me to enter the nationwide competition for the job and then allow the Lord to work out the details.

"Well, I've just received notification from the Headquarters that I was selected for the position. On July 12, I report for work."

Graduation day ended, and I began making preparations to move to Washington. I was scared. Yet I knew God was in it and that I could cling to the words of Paul who said, "I can do all things in him who strengthens me" (Phil. 4:13 Conf. Version).

The night before I left, I knelt by the bed I grew up in, for the last time in only God knew how long, and I committed my Mom to the Lord, asking Him to release me from any anxiety I might still have regarding her salvation.

I knew peace in my heart, then, regarding Mom; God was indeed in charge, and His plan for her was being worked out. Our family would be one in Christ. What I had no way of knowing was that He intended to use me as the instrument, as He had with Dad and Margaret. And it's a good thing He didn't tell me, or I would have blown it for sure.

The next morning our family prayed, embraced, and tear-fully said goodbye. I stopped at Holy Cross for early Mass. God had used many people and Christian communities to awaken my awareness of His love, but now my eyes were opened to the fulness of His presence in my Catholic faith. The service was so intensely beautiful that it was as if the Lord was showing me the depths of worship attainable in the most familiar liturgy. And when at the end Father extended the final blessing, the words He spoke seemed directed at me.

"Go in peace to love and serve the Lord."

"Thanks be to God," I responded.

Nothing more could be said. In a theater the curtain would close and appreciative applause would permeate the air, yet this was Church, and we're not supposed to—I just couldn't resist; when the last person exited through the doors, I rose, lifted my arms, and obeyed the impulse. Go ahead, Larry, "Clap your hands!"

A taxi at the curb behind me emitted a particularly annoyed beep, and I came back to the present with a thump! Giving my Bible a squeeze, I turned and crossed the street to my office. I still couldn't believe it all. Shaking my head, all I could say was, "Thanks be to God!"